1

MW00806953

To all the victims and survivors of Domestic Violence, Rape and Sexual Assault: It's not your fault! Get out while you still can. Let's stop the violence!

-Tanisha M. Bagley

A PrintHouse Books; Non-Fiction Title

PRINTHOUSE BOOKS PRESENTS

THE PRICE OF LOVE

One woman's journey through Domestic Violence.

BASED ON A TRUE STORY

NON-FICTION
2nd Edition.

TANISHA M. BAGLEY

VIP INK Publishing Group, Incorporated

Atlanta, GA.

The Price of Love   by T.Bagley; Second Edition

© Copyright 2004 Bagley Publishing.

All rights reserved. No part of this publication may be reproduced, stored in a retrieval system, or transmitted, in any form or by any means, electronic, mechanical, photocopying, recording, or otherwise, without the written prior permission of the author.

Paperback Isbn – 978-0-9886428-6-7

PRINTHOUSE BOOKS, Atlanta, GA.

Published 2-26-2013

www.PrintHouseBooks.com

Library of Congress Cataloging-in-Publication data

Tanisha M. Bagley

The Price of Love; One woman's tedious journey through domestic violence/T.Bagley

1.Non-fiction 2.Domestic Violence 3.Sexual Assault 4. Rape

PRINTED IN THE UNITED STATES OF AMERICA

A PrintHouse Books; Non-Fiction Title

Dedicated to My Baby Brother,
Linda, Mary & Helen;
Rest in Peace… I Love You all and I Thank God for all
his blessings.

Tanisha M. Bagley

The Price of Love

Second Edition

PRINTHOUSE BOOKS.

Bagley Publishing

A PrintHouse Books; Non-Fiction Title

Table of Contents:

Chapter 1: "Family Secrets"

Every now and then a cold sweat wakes me up in the middle of the night. I sit up gasping for air with my arms over my head—trying to protect myself from an invisible assailant like the one that had victimized me for the past 15 years. The sound of my own heartbeat drumming in my chest only intensifies the fear I feel. Instinctively, I run to my children's bedrooms to make sure they're OK. They are. The three of them are sleeping peacefully under the down comforters and bedspreads they got last Christmas. For them, the world is a safe place.

I survey each room, and they're all empty. But the fear is still there. It never goes away. As I try to close my eyes and fall back into wakeful fits of sleep, I can find no comfort. There is never any peace in knowing that somewhere he's still out there. Even my daydreams are filled with anguish and the memory of a man who for years beat me mercilessly. The scars and bruises on my body have long since healed, but the lacerations on my heart and mind are beyond repair.

"Ladies, tonight represents the first night of the rest of your life. You are no longer victims—you are survivors! The worst is behind you, and from this point on, we are going to help you reclaim your life; reclaim your identity and reclaim your future!"

Whitney looked at the face of each woman in the group and remembered how she had felt several years ago, the first time she came to the group. She had made the first step of seeking professional help and counseling after surviving 10 long years of abuse at the hands of her now ex-husband. There were 12 people in her group, and her first night in counseling, she didn't say a word. But she came back week after week until she finally had the strength to talk about what had happened to her. The L.I.P.S. (Living In Peace & Safety) Group had been around for more than 13 years, and had literally helped save Whitney's life. Although her ex-husband was finally in prison for sexual assault, rape and felonious restraint (a lesser charge for kidnapping), against her, she still was left with the challenge of rebuilding her life and restoring her self-esteem. Starting over was not an easy task.

But tonight, Whitney stood proudly at the front of the room—looking into the faces of women who had faced the same kind of abuse and neglect that she had suffered for so long. She had begun her healing process five years after her abuser went to prison. And now, she had dedicated her life to helping other domestic violence and abuse survivors heal and start their lives over again.

Whitney had been a L.I.P.S. facilitator for almost two years, and this was her way of reaching out to help others and giving back to the community.

"My name is Whitney Jordan Little, and I am a survivor of domestic violence. When I was 14, I met and fell in love with my boyfriend who would eventually become my husband. Tonight I stand before you—a proud survivor—after enduring more than 10 years of physical, sexual, mental, emotional, verbal and financial abuse. Most people think that you can only be abused if you're weak or have low self-esteem, but that's not true. There's also the misconception that unless you've got black eyes and broken bones that you're not really being abused. That's not true either. Being a part of this organization will allow the healing process to begin and the educational process to continue. I want to congratulate each of you for making one of the most courageous decisions you'll ever make to take back control of your life. Each of you is a survivor, and that's definitely something to be proud of. Give yourselves a hand!"

The women in the group looked around at each other smiling and erupted into loud and boisterous applause. Yes, tonight was a step in the right direction for each of them.

One young woman in the group seemed a bit nervous and frustrated. When the applause settled down, she raised her hand and spoke. "Whitney, I have a question. Actually, it's more like a concern. My ex-boyfriend cracked three of my ribs and split the side of my head open with a beer bottle. He's in jail now, but I just know that the system is going to let him out sooner rather than later. Every day, I am scared for my life. I don't mean any harm, but I'm not really here for a motivational speech. I want to know how to start my life over again. I want to know how to keep from ending up in another abusive relationship—because the next time, I might not be lucky enough to make it out alive."

"Do you mind telling us your name," Whitney asked.

"My name is Toni," she said.

"Toni, we're not just here to motivate you. But one of the things we do is applaud you for taking bold and courageous steps toward improving your future. L.I.P.S. is obviously not a social club. Nobody in this room is here by choice—I guarantee that. We're all here because someone took away our control, took away our power, took advantage of us and abused us; and now we're taking it all back.

I'm pretty sure that we all have days where we wake up afraid that it's not really over. That comes with the territory. But I have good news. Each of us has the power and ability within ourselves to take our lives—and our children's lives—back again."

Another woman in her mid-40s raised her hand.

"Excuse me Whitney, but I think I remember hearing about your case."

Whitney nodded and asked, "What do you remember, uhh?"

"Oh, I'm sorry. My name is Karen, and I'm also a survivor of domestic violence. My husband terrorized my kids and me for six years. One Friday night I just decided I'd had enough. I made arrangements to get a job in another state. I only told my parents and my sister where I was going. And one night when he was working late, I packed up our belongings, and me and my kids got the hell out of there." There was familiar and nervous laughter in the room.

She continued, "But anyway, I think I remember reading about your case in the newspaper, and it was also covered on the evening news. Usually you don't hear a lot about the victims—I mean, survivors—in domestic violence cases, but you were so open and honest about what happened to you, it's like you became the voice for domestic violence. I remember hearing your story and thinking what a brave young woman you must be. And now, I'm sitting right here in front of you. I know you're supposed to stick to the agenda, but I think it would be really helpful if everyone knew your story. You're a wonderful example for domestic violence survivors everywhere."

Whitney nodded her head again and said, "Sometimes I feel like the voice for women around the world that want and need to escape. I want to show them that I understand, and that they can get out too. My story is a familiar one to many of you. I'm more than happy to share my ordeal, because sharing has the power to heal, and that's what we're all here for. Each week, we'll each share more and more about what we survived, how we survived, and what the future holds for us. Let's take some time and introduce ourselves to each other now. But for anyone who wants to read more about my life, there are copies of my book, magazine and newspaper articles in the back of the room."

My mother had me when she was 17 years old. My biological father was 20 at the time. My grandmother raised me from the time I was a baby. I guess she felt that my mother wasn't prepared to raise me. I went to pre¬school in the Bronx, New York, and I can only remember my mom having me for two years at the time—which took a big toll on me.

I grew up with three generations living under one roof. My grandmother moved to Virginia to take care of her mother. My mom was back and forth living in different states. I remember not understanding why all my friends and cousins lived with their mom and I didn't. But fortunately, I had a real close relationship with both of my grandmothers.

I grew up in a household with my cousin who was mentally and physically retarded. She had a birth defect and was the product of severe alcohol abuse by her mother. My grandmother was divorced—which I didn't find out until much later. She too was a survivor of domestic violence. I didn't know much about my grandfather. And nobody ever really mentioned him.

Our family was full of secrets. Everything was hush-hush, which is the environment where violence and abuse thrives. My family never discussed the things that were wrong. And only when we were older did we find out the source of some of the skeletons that have continued to haunt our family today.

My grandmother's boyfriend sexually molested my mother, but nobody ever said anything. He would ask to touch them in certain places for a quarter. That really did a lot of emotional damage to my mom. On one hand, they were grateful to have a man around who actually provided for the household and helped them survive. But on the other hand, he was molesting and abusing the children that were in the house. This was a strange man who came along and lent a helping hand to keep the family together, but he also was quietly tearing the family apart.

My grandmother endured a lot of abuse before she finally left. My mother endured a lot before she finally left. I endured a lot before I finally left. The pattern was evident, and history was clearly repeating itself. The skeletons kept resurfacing, but nobody said anything for years.

I know that my mother and grandmother were very close. As a matter of fact, when we moved from New York to Virginia, we moved into a trailer right behind my grandmother's house. If anything ever went wrong, my mother would run back to her mom. That's how close they were. If things weren't going well in her marriage, she would run back home to her mother.

I don't know a lot about my father. During the time that we spent together, we were very close, and I think my mom may have been jealous of that. She never got the chance to experience a loving and normal relationship with her father; she suffered at the hands of an abusive man in the house. I can see why she would envy me.

I only spent a couple of years with my biological father. My mom and dad were together at one point, but they weren't married. Then my mom left my dad and married another man—her first husband. He was from North Carolina. They only stayed together about a year because he abused her. He had threatened and pulled a gun on her in the past. Time and experience had proven that abuse only gets worse with time. When my mother was eight months pregnant, her first husband beat her so severely that she lost the baby. In a fit of jealous rage, he assaulted her when she came home from a night out with her friends. The doctors did everything they could, but to no avail. It was a baby boy—the son she had always wanted. That was the last straw, and she finally left the relationship.

When I was young, my biological father and I spent a lot of time together going to movies and eating out. I knew my mom was jealous of the relationship we had and would do anything to destroy it. At one point when she left him, I felt like she was doing it out of spite—to punish the two of us for finding the kind of love that had eluded her for so long.

This only strained the relationship between my mother and I even more. In my young eyes, my dad was wonderful, and he could do no wrong. Admittedly, I was young and didn't understand everything that was going on. But even at that tender age, I couldn't see any valid reason why she would leave him. He didn't beat her. He hadn't abused her in any way. He went to work every day, and he provided for our family. With her first

husband, I knew he had beaten her, threatened her and verbally abused her; and she had lost her baby because of him. But with my dad, I just felt like she didn't want me to have a good relationship with him. Misery loves company, so she left him too.

Mom started seeing her second husband while she was still with my dad in New York. And I can remember the first time we met him. She took me and my cousin Veronica—whom she took in and raised as her own daughter—over to his house. She told my dad that we were going to church.

And we did. We all went to church together. My cousin, my mom, her new boyfriend, and me. She would eventually marry him. Apparently he had enough money and gave her enough materialistic things to make it worth her while. We met his family and spent time with them. I remember my mother instructing me not to tell my father.

Her new boyfriend won us over by giving us gifts. It's easy to influence children, so his gifts bought our approval. But I still wanted my family to stay together. I knew exactly what was going on—and what my mother was doing. But I didn't say anything, because I didn't want to hurt my dad.

At the time, my mother was working for New York Financial Bank, and her boyfriend Keith was a delivery driver. There was a lot of covering up, hiding and sneaking around. We would go out to visit him in Staten Island. And we even went to church and had dinner together like a real family. Keith seemed like a good guy—even though he was dating a woman who already had a family and was committed—at least partially—to another man. Keith was clean-cut, well dressed and attractive. He had a large house and lived with his mother, whom he was taking care of. He had a good job and made good money, and I guess my mother felt financially secure with him.

My mother just always wanted more. Keith was able to give her money and jewelry and things like that. We never went without anything, and Keith gave us lots of gifts. Even though my dad took good care of us too, I knew my mother was still going to leave him. She just wanted a man who could give her more.

I remember the day when the relationship ended. I felt like I had betrayed my mother. We had gone out to wash clothes at the corner Laundromat, and she sent me back to the house to get some laundry detergent. My father was standing at the sink doing the dishes when I walked in the house, and he asked me if my mother was seeing somebody else. I told him "yes," because I felt he needed to hear the truth from me.

My choice was the lesser of two evils; be honest with my father and betray my mother, or keep silent and continue living a lie. My mother came home to check on me and we went back to the Laundromat together. I told my mother about the conversation with my dad.

The next thing I remember is that my mother was quickly packing up our belongings and throwing everything into garbage bags. I was only about nine years old, but I recall my mother's boyfriend sending a cab to pick us up in the Bronx and bring us to Staten Island. There was so much activity in the house, and it was the only time I remember my dad showing force toward me.

He grabbed me by my arm and said, "You told her, didn't you?" I was so afraid. I felt like them breaking up and us having to move out was all my fault. I never heard much from my father after that. I felt guilty for a very long time and carried those emotions with me for years.

I spent my 4th and 5th grade years in New York. About a year later, my mother got pregnant with my younger sister. She and Keith had been together for some time, but still hadn't gotten married. After a while, they decided to move from New York to Virginia. That summer, we went to visit, and I ended up staying behind with my grandmother while my parents returned to New York to sell our house.

I resented being left behind again. I spent another two years with my grandmother before I eventually moved back in with my mom and stepfather. I spent my childhood feeling like a visitor in my own mother's house. I always felt that she chose men over me. Her life and lifestyle were more important than having me with her.

Both my sister and I lived with our grandmother for a few years. My grandmother was very controlling and had a lot of influence on my mother's life. At first my stepdad was OK with it, but after a while, it began to wear on him. It wasn't until later in the relationship that he realized how controlling and possessive my grandmother was, and how much control she had over their household. Nothing happened unless my grandmother said so. That would eventually tear their marriage apart. My mother had never been one to make a whole lot of decisions on her own. She basically just did what other people told her to do.

When I was in 10th grade, the tension in our home escalated to a whole new level. By this time, I had watched my mother get in and out of various relationships that weren't really good for her. She started cheating regularly; first with a co-worker, and then with other men from around our town. Even after she married my stepfather, it seemed like she was never satisfied.

Although we had a house, car and nice furniture, it wasn't enough. My biological father was good to her. My stepfather was good to her, but she just wasn't satisfied. It sometimes seemed like she was looking for trouble. It was like she was more comfortable in the chaos than in the calm.

The birth of my baby brother, Donnie, brought a little more joy into my mother's life. He was like the missing part of her that she had been searching for all these years. Maybe it was because of the baby boy she had lost years before during her pregnancy, or maybe it was because she just needed someone else to love her. But Donnie could do no wrong—and my sister and I resented him for that. Somehow he managed to get all the love and care from our mom that we never could.

Growing up and observing my own family helped me determine how my life would be different. Knowing how badly my mother had been hurt, and knowing how badly her on-again, off-again relationships had hurt our family, I decided that if I ever had children, I would stay in the relationship—no matter what. That decision would later cost me dearly, but I was willing to pay the price to keep my family intact.

I had seen and experienced the hurt that my father felt by my mother's other relationships. I knew how it felt to think that my own mother didn't love me as much as she did some man she hardly knew. As a child, that practically broke my heart.

I just decided that my life was going to be different. And I decided that I would do whatever I had to do to keep my family together. Cheating wasn't an option, and divorce wasn't an option.

But everything I tried so hard to avoid, I would eventually encounter. Everything that I held sacred would eventually cause me to suffer. I desperately did not want to become a statistic. But despite all my efforts to make my marriage work, I ended up in the very place I was trying so desperately to avoid.

Nothing is ever what it seems. In my eyes, my biological father was a wonderful man who could do no wrong. And my mother was selfish and materialistic— hell-bent on destroying our family. But in reality, my father was not the perfect example of manhood that I had imagined him to be. Nor was my mother a glutton for punishment. They both had problems of their own. And they both had valid reasons for the decisions they made.

The problem with keeping secrets and skeletons in the closet is that one day they eventually get out and haunt individuals who know nothing about them. Skeletons and family secrets were abundant in our family.

I thought that my father had stayed with my mother purely out of love. I believed it was because he wanted to keep his family together. And that was partly true. But the other part was guilt. He stayed and endured her infidelity, because he too had gone astray.

The secret was one of those things that everybody whispered about, but nobody spoke aloud. I guess the situation was a little too close for comfort. My father had cheated on my mother. But not with some strange woman from across town, or with some long-lost girlfriend. He cheated with my mother's cousin; a girl that had grown up in the house with her—and treated her like a sister.

That kind of betrayal breeds anger and contempt deeper than the mind can imagine. It helped to explain some of my mother's resentment and some of her brokenness.

Sometimes it seemed like my mother couldn't commit to anyone or anything—not even her own children. But instead of questioning why she acted this way, I just blamed her for not loving me enough... until I got older. Her mother's boyfriend had molested her when she was a child. He would fondle them and touch them in inappropriate places—right under his girlfriend's nose. She was being treated like a prostitute before she was old enough to drive. My mother's first encounters with men were marked by sexually abusive and controlling behaviors.

She developed a natural and understandable fear of intimacy. She feared men. She feared love. She feared that her own mother couldn't protect her. And she feared that the individuals she loved would eventually betray her. She was right.

I now realize that my mother didn't feel safe anywhere—not even in her own home. She had been hurt and betrayed twice by family members in ways that could never be repaired or restored. She had a right to fear relationships and commitments. She had a right to be bitter. She couldn't have a normal, intimate relationship, because she didn't really know what one looked like.

After my mom and dad separated, it hurt me that my father didn't try to keep in contact with me—even though he knew exactly where I was. Ironically, for a while, my dad lived with my aunt (my mom's sister) and her husband while they got back on their feet and started a new life on their own.

It became clear he simply wasn't interested in being a father to me. I don't think fathers truly understand how much damage they do in a child's life by not being there. Not having your father leaves a void that nothing else can fill. Growing up, we had been so close and spent so

much time together, and then nothing… not even a phone call or a card on my birthday.

Sometimes I think about all the things we missed out on doing together.

I think that little girls learn about relationships from how their fathers treat their mothers—and how their fathers treat them. When a man takes care of his responsibilities to love and nurture his little girl, she's likely to attract someone who loves and nurtures her in a relationship.

But if she never had a father, then she spends her entire adult life seeking a father figure—when what she really needs is a man who loves and cherishes her. Fathers build self-esteem in little girls and let them know what is (or is not) acceptable behavior from a man. Good fathers give their little girls a sense of safety and protection. Good fathers protect their little girls from harm and let them know what harm looks like—so they can recognize it from a distance. Not having that constant influence around can be devastating.

Chapter 2: "First Love"

In 1988, I was only 14 years old. Within one year of meeting my high school sweetheart and future husband, I would become the victim of physical, mental, verbal, emotional, financial and sexual abuse; and undergo the first of three abortions. There was a time when we were madly and deeply in love. But a lot of time and a lot of violence separates where we were then from where we are now.

Kevin Little and I both lived in a small town. He was in Snow Hill, VA, and I was in Mineral Springs, VA. When I first met him and realized who he was, he was headed to high school, and I was finishing my last year in junior high. We ended up going to the same high school and having some of the same friends.

I was a quiet student who made good grades and did what was expected of me. I was a self-described "good girl"—a "goody two-shoes" who had nothing but a promising future ahead of me. I was finally living a stable life with my mother and stepfather, and my grandmothers who were nearby. I had a few close friends—who also happened to be my cousins—and I was looking forward to going to high school the following year.

On the weekends, my friends and I would talk on the phone and hang out at each other's houses. In a small town like ours, there wasn't much more to do. We weren't old enough to drive yet, and even if we had been, none of us could afford our own car.

Summers in 1987 were fun-filled vacations from homework, teachers and classes. We played in each other's yards and near the woods until the outside lights came on, ending our day's play and beckoning us to come inside for dinner. Then we called each other on the phone after dinner to talk some more. Summers in 1987 were carefree, the way teenage years were meant to be.

That would be my last carefree summer. It was the last time I would deal with "teenage issues" instead of "adult issues." As I look back over the last 15 years of my life, I realize how much I would have embraced the summer of 1987 if I had known how important it would become in my life and that it would be my last pleasant memory of childhood.

That year represented the end of my youth. It would be the last time I didn't worry about being raped or getting pregnant—by force. It would be the last time I didn't worry about hiding cuts and bruises or getting punched in the face. That year would be the last time I felt safe for a very, very long time.

It wasn't until that first week in high school—fall 1988—that Kevin and I met and were formally introduced. A mutual friend of ours had given Kevin my telephone number. I was a freshman, and this was Kevin's sophomore year. I was 14 years old, and he was

15. I distinctly remember that I didn't like Kevin—and that's the God's honest truth. I thought he was arrogant, conceited and full of himself. He took "overly confident" to a whole new level. Kevin was the only guy in school who was dressed up every single day. He wore a shirt, tie, dress slacks and dress shoes. He never wore sneakers to class. He only wore sneakers when he played basketball. Everyday he was dressed to kill.

But the more time I spent with Kevin, the more I realized that he was funny; he was really sweet and really kind. From my perspective, his arrogance turned out to be confidence and self-assurance. I figured that this guy was going somewhere in life. He had a love for basketball. He had a love for acting. He was on the debate team. He liked political science and dreamed of becoming a lawyer or going into politics. So, he came off to be very intelligent. He was a pretty good student. His grades were good, and he was just popular and Mr. Charismatic.

As far as the basketball team, Kevin was one of the main guys on the team. Basically, he was a jock. But his popularity and basketball status weren't what attracted me to him. It was his character and how he came across to me. Kevin was very clean-cut—just like my stepfather.

He was polished and poised. I knew my parents would like him. I thought I had picked a winner. In the beginning, Kevin pursued me and showed me respect. I was the sole object of his affection. That type of behavior really gets a 14-year-old girl's attention. The more we talked, the better I got to know him. He was humorous and very loving. And that's how he won me over; he was my first love.

Kevin was my first boyfriend. I ate, slept, and drank him. He was the first person I thought about in the morning and the last person I thought about at night. I couldn't wait to go to school everyday just to see him. We saw each other between classes, we didn't even eat lunch at school; we just spent all the time we could together getting to know each other better. We immediately became best friends. I never had a lot of girlfriends—other than my cousins—so Kevin became my best friend. We were inseparable.

It was nothing for us to spend the entire day together, just hanging out and having fun. We would go into town or go to the lake. Then he'd come over to my house and spend time with my family and me, and his parents would pick him up in the evenings.

My mother liked him because he was charming, charismatic and clean-cut. Kevin really played up that charismatic role to my mother. He was just so charming that he easily won her over. My stepfather liked him OK, but was always kind of leery of him; like most fathers are when their daughters start dating.

One afternoon Kevin and I were sitting on the front porch. It was fairly cool, although winter hadn't fully arrived. In the yard, there were little signs that cold weather was on the way. There were a few flowers left alongside the porch and some brown leaves that fell out of the trees and lined the yard. Kevin seemed distant that day—like his mind was a million miles away. "It happened again," he said. "What happened," I asked. One of the things I loved the most about our relationship was that we could tell each other everything.

"The fighting. It's like they never stop fighting," he said. "After all these years, I can't believe that they are still fighting and arguing." Kevin's parents had gotten married early—like most couples did in those days. Both of them were college-educated, hard-working professionals. His mother seemed to be poised and confident—definitely not the type of woman who would sit back and do nothing while some man beat on her. But looks can be deceiving. She worked for the State of Virginia, and had been a long-time employee. His father was a business owner and part-time instructor at the local community college.

Kevin said, "I came home late from basketball practice and I could hear my mother screaming for help. When I walked in, I saw my mom on the floor on her knees with her arms wrapped around my dad's legs while he beat her on her back with a belt. She was begging and pleading with him not to hit her again—and to spare her life. I've never seen anything so pathetic. I looked at my mom and her eyes seemed to be pleading for help. I just went into my bedroom and turned on my radio. I didn't want to hear them fighting anymore.

"The way he treated her was inhumane. My mother goes to work every day; she's got 12 people working under her, and when she comes home, she has to beg him not to hit her. The other night, I stopped him from chasing her outside with a gun. I wanted to involve the police, but that would have just set my dad off all over again. His philosophy is: 'What happens behind closed doors stays behind closed doors.'"

Kevin picked up a twig by his foot and broke it into tiny little pieces. We just sat there beside each other in silence. I knew Kevin was still thinking about his parents and whether or not they would be fighting again when he got home that night. I was thinking about how glad I was that Kevin was nothing like his father. I was happy knowing that he would never hit me or abuse our family.

I knew that both my grandmother and mother had suffered at the hands of an abuser, but I was going to break that cycle. I was going to be different. Kevin was smart, funny, intelligent, charming and well-mannered. He and I were going to have a great family and a wonderful future together.

Kevin's parents presented a good façade. They always looked like they should be happy. They were one of a few families in their community that had already achieved the "American Dream." They appeared to have the perfect life. Both parents worked full time and had good jobs. They had two all-American sons; both were intelligent, athletic and popular. They attended family gatherings and sporting events together. They were supportive of Kevin and his brother Kendall in every way—attending their basketball, baseball and football games together and giving them everything they wanted and needed.

To say that Kevin and Kendall were spoiled is an understatement. Kevin's parents gave him and his brother everything they wanted. They wore name brand clothes all the time. They shopped for new clothes every season and shopped out of town, so no one would have on the same clothes they had. They were going to get brand new cars when they turned 16 and got their driver's licenses. They were rotten to the core. If Kevin and Kendall wanted it—they got it. In their parents' eyes, those two boys could do no wrong. Even when they were wrong, they were right.

But I guess you never really know what's going on behind closed doors. Kevin's family looked perfect from the outside, but in reality, Mrs. Little was struggling to keep her family together. Money, education and big houses don't make families immune from violence and abuse.

It's so easy to stereotype the kind of people we think are at risk for abuse, but no one ever falls in love with an abuser. That part of the personality doesn't show up until later—when it's not as easy to simply walk away.

My mother's voice broke my concentration. It was getting dark, and Kevin and I had been sitting on the porch holding hands and talking for hours. "Whitney, it's getting late. We've got church tomorrow morning. You two need to say goodnight. Kevin, are your parents coming to get you, or do you need a ride home?"

"Yes, ma'am," he said. "Thank you for asking, but my parents should be here any minute." He was so polite.

There was so much to like about him, but there are always two sides to every story.

It had been several months since we started dating, and our grades were beginning to slip because of the enormous amount of time we spent together. Kevin and I lost interest in everything else except each other. Both sets of parents became concerned that we were spending so much time together, but there's not much you can say to two teenagers in love.

They tried to regulate the amount of time we spent together, and that was disastrous. Kevin and I just cried in each other's arms when we found out that our parents were trying to separate us. We were like a modern-day Romeo and Juliet—determined to be together one way or another. When our parents realized how serious we were, they agreed to let us continue seeing each other if we agreed to concentrate more on school and improve our grades. We tried, but our efforts availed little, and didn't last very long.

Kevin told me that from the first time he laid eyes on me, he knew I was going to be his wife. We were everything to each other. All my time, energy and focus were on Kevin. And all his time, energy and focus were on me. We secretly talked until 2:00 or 3:00 o'clock in the morning every day—even on school nights. Kevin had a lot of flexibility with his parents. Because he was a good kid—popular, athletic and doing OK in school—he didn't have a curfew or any strict rules to follow, which resulted in his total lack of respect for authority and structure in his life. I—on the other hand—had a strict curfew and couldn't go out as much as he could, but we made the best out of the time we did have together. For the most part, we were both good kids, and we weren't doing anything wrong, so our parents let us keep seeing each other more and more. There wasn't anything sexual in our relationship, we just spent that entire first year falling in love and getting to know everything about each other.

People always ask victims and survivors of domestic violence why they don't just leave—or how can they stay with a man who treats them so badly. But that's one of the biggest misconceptions about abusive relationships. No one falls in love with an abuser. I fell in love with my best friend. He was funny, caring, kind and charismatic. That's the personality he sold me. That's who I believed he was. I had never seen anything in his personality other than this wonderful young man who he allowed me to see. Although I knew there were some issues with his mom and dad, I never saw any of those tendencies in Kevin. I had no reason to think that he would ever lay a hand on me. I had no reason to think that he would ever do anything to destroy the perfect life we had planned together. And by the time I realized who he really was, I was already deeply in love with him.

When you love someone, it's difficult to just turn those feelings on and off like a faucet. Love doesn't work that way. I wanted our relationship to work, and I wanted us to be happy together. Love is unconditional. No matter what someone that you love says or does, your heart makes you want to keep on loving them. No victim of abuse likes being abused. No individual in a domestic violence situation plans or desires to be in that situation. At some point in the relationship, there was kindness and tenderness and love.

When I look at myself in the mirror, I know that I'm one of the fortunate ones because I actually made it out alive. So many others do not. Based on my own experiences, I'm taking the lessons that I learned, and I'm using that information to help other individuals— particularly young women—to recognize the warning signs of an abusive partner. My goal is to help others avoid making the mistakes I made. In domestic violence relationships, somebody's life is at stake.

As I look back over the past 15 years of my life, I see a lot of things that I would have done differently. Hindsight has 20/20 vision. But there were just a lot of things I didn't know. I wasn't informed about healthy relationships, about men, about sex, or even about my own body.

The conversation my mother had with me about the 'birds and the bees' and what my body was experiencing at age 14, lasted less than one minute. I had gone into the bathroom and noticed that there were large drops of blood on my panties. The only thing I knew was what I had heard at school. I had a lot of wrong information about starting my menstrual cycle, and I was equipped with a lot of false rumors about sex. So, I went to my mom, hoping that since my period had arrived, she would clear up some of the misunderstandings for me.

I remember going to my mother's bedroom where she had been taking a nap. I told her that I thought my period was starting. She said, "Just go put a pad on." That was the end of the conversation. She rolled over and went back to sleep. Everything else I learned about my body and my sexuality, I learned on my own. That's one of the biggest mistakes a parent can make is to not let their children learn the truth about life from them. Schoolyard sex education is deadly.

I didn't know that the onset of my menstrual cycle meant that I was now capable of getting pregnant. I didn't realize that sex could have such severe consequences.

And I didn't understand that although my body was ready to have a child, I was not.

In spite of the difficulties we encountered in our relationship e.g. parental disapproval, falling grades, etc., Kevin and I made it through our first year of dating, and to us, everything was wonderful. We now thought we were mature enough to elevate our relationship to the next level. But we weren't going to be careless or reckless like other teens and have sex on the spur of the moment. We talked about our relationship and planned our first intimate encounter.

The entire week leading up to our first "big night," was filled with nervousness and excitement. In my mind, having sex with Kevin would solidify our relationship. We were already in love, but this would be the final step to secure our relationship. We were going to be together forever. Because Kevin was a year older than me, I trusted that he was more knowledgeable and more experienced than I was. In reality, we were both virgins—and both too young to understand what we were getting into. He didn't know any more than I did.

It just so happened that both my parents were scheduled to work on Saturday and I was at home babysitting, so Kevin and I had some time to ourselves. I put a cartoon video in the VCR for the kids to watch, and Kevin and I went to my bedroom. I wanted this night to be special.

This was the moment I had dreamed about. Kevin and I were about to make the most important decision of our lives and physically commit ourselves to each other for life. Kevin took off his shirt and pulled me close to him. He kissed me once and hugged me. We lay down on the bed and he undressed me. I was embarrassed about being naked, and I had never seen a penis before. I wasn't sure what to do next.

The TV soap operas made sex seem magical. My first time seemed awkward, and I wasn't sure if Kevin knew what he was doing either. He climbed on top of me, and I felt him go inside me. He was breathing hard and grunting. I just lay there with him between my legs. Three minutes later, he was done, and I felt like a woman. Little did I know, I was also pregnant.

We had talked about our first time being special. We talked about how we felt about each other. We talked about our future together. But we never talked about the consequences of our actions. And I don't think either one of us really understood what we were getting into. We didn't use protection, and I definitely was not on any type of birth control. We were just going to hope for the best. That was our plan, and it failed.

Kevin and I spent the entire summer together. There was little outside interference, so we were able to solely focus on each other. We spent all of our time at the lake and making plans for our future. The summers were always happy times for us.

A few weeks before school started, we were both getting ready for a new year. I went to the local shops to purchase school clothes, whereas Kevin went out of town to the malls and men's specialty stores. My clothes were "off the rack," but his were "one of a kind."

It wasn't until school started that I noticed Kevin's personality beginning to change. Kevin wanted me all to himself, and seeing me talking to anyone else made him jealous. At first, I was flattered. Later, it became a problem. He accused me of seeing other guys, which wasn't true. But in retaliation, he started flirting with other girls, and that drove me crazy.

Now that we had started having sex, Kevin felt as though I "belonged" to him. He started acting very possessive and controlling. He wanted to know every move I made. For the first time, he accused me of lying, and it became apparent that he didn't trust a word I said anymore.

Kevin and I had been at odds all week, and I was tired of defending myself to him. I'll never forget—it was a Friday—we were having our first full-fledged argument, and things were getting pretty bad. We just weren't getting along. That afternoon after school, we were still yelling about the disagreements of the day. Normally, we would have spent several more hours on the phone, talking until the wee hours of the morning. But this day, our conversation ended around 4:00 p.m. I yelled into the phone and slammed it down while he was still talking. Finally, I'd had enough. As soon as the phone hit the receiver, a large amount of blood and water gushed down my leg onto the floor. It concerned me, because I didn't know what was happening. But I didn't do anything about it. I immediately called Kevin back and told him what had just happened. We were both confused and unaware of the severity of the situation. But at least this gave us an opportunity to talk and make up.

When my mom got home from work, I told her what was happening. I didn't let her know how serious it was, and she didn't seem overly concerned. I figured that the heavy bleeding was just part of my usual menstrual cycle. For the next 10 hours, I was constantly in and out of the bathroom urinating blood.

By 2:00 a.m., I was still bleeding—passing heavy "grape-like" clots of blood, water and tissue. In actuality, I was hemorrhaging; slowly bleeding to death. By now I was afraid, and I knew that something was definitely wrong.

"Mom! I think something's wrong," I said. "Look! There's blood all over my clothes, and it's all over my bedroom floor too. I've been bleeding really heavily since late this afternoon. I thought it was my period, but something's wrong! What do you think is wrong with me," I asked.

Instinctively, my mother already knew what was wrong. It was the first thing she asked me. "Whitney, have you been having sex?"

"No," I lied.

"I'm going to ask you again… have you been having sex? You might as well tell the truth because I'm taking you to the doctor, and if you're pregnant, I'm going to find out."

Pregnant? The thought never crossed my mind.

"Yes ma'am. Kevin and I had sex a couple of times, but I'm not pregnant," I said. "We'll see… get your coat on and let's go." We picked up my grandmother first, and then headed straight to the hospital.

When we arrived at the emergency room, I was diagnosed with a "mole pregnancy" and immediately sent to an operating room for an emergency D&C. A D&C (dilation and curettage) of the uterus is a pregnancy termination procedure. A small vacuum device is inserted into the uterus, under anesthesia, to abort the pregnancy and remove fetal tissue. All of this was new to me. I was terrified and not certain if I was going to live or die. This is what we found out about my pregnancy:

Molar "Mole" Pregnancy-- Molar pregnancies are an uncommon and very frightening complication of pregnancy. The formal medical term for a molar pregnancy is "hydatidiform mole." Simply put, a molar pregnancy is an abnormality of the placenta (afterbirth), caused by a problem when the egg and sperm join together at fertilization. The following is a brief review of this subject. (Hill)

Types of Molar Pregnancy

There are two types of molar pregnancy, complete and partial. Complete molar pregnancies have only placental parts (there is no baby), and form when the sperm fertilizes an empty egg. Because the egg is empty, no baby is formed. The placenta grows and produces the pregnancy hormone, called HCG, so the patient thinks she is pregnant. Unfortunately, an ultrasound (sometimes called a sonogram) will show that there is no baby, only placenta. A partial mole occurs when two sperm fertilize an egg. Instead of forming twins, something goes wrong, leading to a pregnancy with an abnormal fetus and an abnormal placenta. The baby has too many chromosomes and almost always dies in the uterus. (Hill)

My mother called Kevin and his parents to let them know what was going on. Kevin and his father showed up at the emergency room around 3:00 a.m. My mom explained what had happened, and amazingly nobody got angry or started yelling. As a matter of fact, our parents forgave us and split the costs of the medical bills. I was both shocked and relieved.

The doctor told me that if I got pregnant again within a year, I could die. We were informed that mole pregnancies could recur—even after a thorough D&C— and cause some type of blood disorder. I learned that recurrent mole pregnancies had the ability to metastasize and spread like cancer, requiring chemotherapy treatment. For the first time, my relationship with Kevin had put my life in jeopardy.

Honestly, I thought the doctor was just saying that to scare Kevin and me, and to keep us from having sex at such an early age. It didn't seem as though anybody wanted us to be together. For the most part, I took the doctor's warnings seriously, but neither of us really believed that I could die. I would later find out that everything the doctor told us was true; it wasn't an attempt to scare us. It was an attempt to save my life.

Mole Pregnancy Follow-up

After evacuating a molar pregnancy it is critically important that the patient see her doctor frequently, as molar pregnancies can recur. Follow-up usually consists of a baseline chest x-ray, review of the pathology specimen, physical examination of the vagina and uterus every two weeks until the uterus returns to normal; then every 3 months for a year, contraception like the pill or shot with no attempt to become pregnant for 1 year, and, most importantly, weekly HCG blood levels until zero then every month for a year. Many women are frustrated when their doctor recommends waiting one year to become pregnant. This is actually important, because a rise in HCG levels may indicate a normal pregnancy when the patient is trying to get pregnant, or a recurrent molar pregnancy, which requires chemotherapy. To avoid this confusion physicians generally recommend a 1-year period without becoming pregnant. (Hill)

Going through this traumatic event only drew Kevin and I closer together. Now that we had faced a crisis together, we were a team. We were a family. Although we were only 15 and 16 years old, we felt as though our relationship was mature since we were dealing with adult issues. Neither of us had learned our lesson, and we didn't heed the warning signals that everyone around us was sending.

Even though the thought of getting pregnant again scared me, I still loved Kevin and wanted to be with him in every way. Nothing and no one was going to get in the way of that.

By now, Kevin and I were both in high school and still very much in love. We had conceived and lost a child together, and there was nothing more we wanted to do than spend every waking moment together healing and nurturing our relationship.

I was a sophomore and Kevin was a junior. And although he was our high school's star basketball player, he decided to quit playing sports to spend more time with me. I never asked him to quit playing basketball— or doing anything he enjoyed—for me. I wanted him to play basketball because I knew that he loved the game. It was like Kevin gave up his dream to make me happy; he would blame me for it the rest of our lives. I had never seen so many people disappointed and angered over one decision in my entire life. Kevin's parents almost had a fit when he told them he wasn't going to play basketball anymore.

They knew without a doubt that he was destined to play in the NBA. But because he was in love with me, he was going to ruin his future—and the dreams they had for him. The coaches were outraged, because they knew their winning season was now in jeopardy. Some of his teammates stopped speaking to him after begging him to come back on the team didn't work. My parents weren't pleased either, because quitting the team meant Kevin would have even more free time to spend with me.

During the fall of 1989, Kevin and I were together more than ever. That's when I first began to see a side of him I never imagined possible. He thought that since he had given up basketball for me, I should give him whatever he wanted—whenever he wanted it. As the weeks went by, he became more and more controlling and started exhibiting very jealous behavior.

He questioned what I wore to school, who my friends were, why I took so long in the bathroom, where I had been if I was out of his sight, and everything else you can imagine. I didn't interpret his behavior as warning signs of an abuser. I just took them as being overly concerned about his girlfriend. After all, we were planning to have a life together. He had a right to know where I was.

Early one Saturday evening, my mom asked me and Kevin to go to the store for her to pick up some things that she needed for dinner. By now, Kevin had his driver's license, so off we went. We loved going to the store together because it allowed us to be alone together and get out of the house.

"Whitney, tell your mother that we're going to a party tonight. I want us to spend some time together. It's been a few weeks since we've been together, and you know what I want."

I was appalled that he would even suggest that we sleep together after I had been given a death sentence if I got pregnant again within a year. I said, "No, I don't want to lie to my mom, and I don't want to go to any party. And we're definitely not gonna have sex. Don't you remember what the doctor told me?"

"I know, but baby, I love you so much," he said. "I just want to be with you. What's wrong with that," he asked.

"Baby, I love you too, but I just don't want to risk getting pregnant again."

"Listen, I know we messed up once, but I'll wear a condom this time. I'll wear a condom and pull out ahead of time. Baby, please! I just want to spend some time with you. Tell your mother we're going to a party tonight. OK?"

"No, no, no. Kevin, I don't want to do this. And I don't want to start fighting either. Just drop it, OK?"

I could tell he was getting agitated with me. "No, it's not OK. I spend all my time with you," he said. "I quit basketball for you. I'm catching hell at home because of you. All I want to do is spend time with you, and you act like you don't want to be with me. Who else are you messing around with? Huh, tell me!"

I took a deep breath and said, "Just cut it out, Kevin. I'm not messing around with anybody. I love you—you know that. I just don't want to go to any stupid party, and I don't think we should still be having sex after what happened. Just take me back home!"

I can still envision in slow motion what happened after that. I remember screaming at Kevin to take me back home, and the next thing I felt was the palm of his hand going across the side of my face. I was stunned. So was he.

Tears streamed down my face like a waterfall. I didn't hear anything else he had to say.

"Oh my God! Baby, I'm so sorry that I hit you. I swear to God, I will never hit you again. I don't know what happened. I just lost it for a minute, but I swear it will never happen again. I was just frustrated because it seemed like you didn't love me anymore, and you acted like you didn't want to be with me. Baby, are you listening to me? I'm so sorry. Please forgive me. I will never hit you again. Did you hear me... honey? I'm sorry. Oh God, please don't tell your parents what happened. I swear, it was a mistake, and I'll never do it again. I'm sorry. I'm so sorry."

I just sat in the passenger's seat crying.

The 10-minute drive back home seemed like forever. Kevin begged for forgiveness the entire time, and I just sat quietly, rubbing my face on the spot his hand had struck me. A thousand thoughts ran through my mind.

'How could he hit me?' As much as Kevin hated what his father was doing to his mother, I couldn't believe he was turning into the same person. He had sworn to me that he would never, ever hit a woman.

He didn't understand his father's behavior and didn't want to be anything like him. Kevin had witnessed firsthand how abuse could destroy a relationship, and he hit me anyway.

By the time he dropped me off in front of my house, I had decided that the entire incident was my fault. He was right. If I had just agreed to tell my mom that we were going to a party together, none of this would have happened. If I had just listened to him, he wouldn't have gotten upset with me. We had already been intimate, so it wasn't like he was forcing me to do something I didn't want to do. He was just trying to find a way for us to spend more time together. I would just be more careful in the future and not make him angry. Kevin and I loved each other, and we wanted to be together. In my mind, this made perfect sense.

Kevin pulled up in front of my driveway and turned off the car headlights. He took my hand in his hand and looked deeply into my eyes.

"Honey, I'm so sorry that I hit you. I swear, it will never happen again. Promise me that you're not going to tell anybody. It was just an accident. You won't ever have to worry about me putting my hands on you again. If your parents find out what happened, they might not let us see each other anymore.

"Just don't say anything. I want you to go straight to the bathroom and put a cold, wet washcloth on your face so the swelling will go down. Then go straight to your room and make sure that nobody sees your face. Don't come out until the swelling and redness have gone down.

"Do you hear me? Remember, if anybody sees it, we might not get to see each other again. Baby, I love you. I promise, it'll never happen again."

He kissed my hand and wiped the tears from my face. Then he kissed me gently on the forehead and watched as I got out of the car and walked back inside the house. By the time I got to the door, I had convinced myself that the entire situation was just a misunderstanding; it really was an accident. But my mother had a completely different reaction.

I had decided to go to the side entrance of the house where the washer and dryer were located to avoid running into anybody. What I didn't know was that my mom had started a load of laundry while she waited for me to come back from the store. When I opened the door, she was standing right in front of me. The first thing she saw was Kevin's handprint on my face.

"Oh my goodness, what happened to your face, Whitney? Did that little punk hit you? What happened?" Before I had a chance to answer, my mom had rushed outside past me to go after Kevin; but thankfully he had already driven off. Instantly, my mom was on the phone with Kevin's parents telling them what happened. Right there on the phone, she ended our relationship for me.

She was enraged. I had never seen my mom so angry. Looking back, I guess part of her anger came from knowing what it was like to be abused. Her mother had suffered through it, she had suffered through it, but she wasn't going to let me make the same mistakes and suffer the same kind of abuse they had endured for so long.

When Kevin's parents confronted him about what happened, he denied it. He looked them straight in the face and lied. That should have convinced me that he wasn't really who he was pretending to be. But I loved him, and I thought he deserved another chance.

The rest of the evening with my mother and grandmother turned into an abuse intervention session. They refused to leave me alone until I understood what kind of person Kevin really was.

"Whitney honey, you don't have to put up with that kind of mess," my grandmother said. "You're a pretty young girl and plenty of nice boys are interested in you. I know you think you're in love with Kevin, but honey, if he hit you once, he'll do it again. Tell her, Anita!"

"Momma's right Whitney. I know you love him, but this boy is nothing but trouble. You've already gotten pregnant, and now he's beating on you. What else has to happen before you realize that he's trouble? You need to get away from him while you still can. He's over there with his parents right now acting like nothing happened. That lying little punk didn't even own up to his mistakes. You deserve better, Whitney. We didn't raise you to put up with no mess from any man. Honey, you're only 15. You've got your whole life ahead of you. Don't let this boy ruin your life.

They talked and talked and talked. But I had stopped listening. Nobody understood Kevin like I did. He had only hit me once, and he swore it would never happen again. I believed him. But my mother and grandmother did not.

For every time someone told me to break up with Kevin and get away from him, Kevin did something else to apologize and make up for his mistake. He sent letters and cards and flowers. He called at least 10 times a day. He begged and pleaded with me to give him another chance. His apologies were incessant, and once again, he won me over. In my heart, I knew he loved me, and that was good enough.

The relationship between my stepfather and me began to deteriorate after I got pregnant and miscarried. To make matters worse, when he found out that Kevin had hit me, he became irate and forbade us to see each other again. But I loved Kevin, and that was all that mattered. I literally didn't speak to my stepfather for more than a year, even though we lived under the same roof. As long as he disapproved of my relationship with Kevin, there was nothing else to talk about. Unfortunately, my mom was torn between her husband and me and didn't know whose side to take. In the end, I won.

It took a couple of weeks to change my mother's mind about Kevin and me. For the first time, I was doing all of the begging and convincing to get her to allow us

to see each other again. I can honestly say I had turned into the master manipulator of the relationship. I guess my mom didn't want our relationship to end up like the relationship between my stepfather and me, so she gave in.

On our first night back together again, my mom allowed Kevin and me to go to a basketball game and dinner. I had every intention of attending, but of course Kevin had a different agenda. We attended the first quarter so that if my mom asked any of her friends whether or not we were there, they would say yes. And then we left. We ended up on an old dirt road that led to a lake.

Kevin parked the car and turned off the ignition. Then he turned to me and put his hand gently on the side of my face. "You are so beautiful," he told me. "I love you so much, Whitney. Please don't ever leave me again. I don't know what I'd do without you."

I looked deep into his eyes and said, "We're gonna be together forever. I love you so much. I don't care what anybody says. You and I were meant for each other." Before long, we were in the backseat making out. Being in love was wonderful. I was with the man of my dreams, and it was the most wonderful feeling in the world.

"Let me make love to you, Whitney. I just want to make up for what happened. I just want to be with you."

"Come on, Kevin. You know what the doctor said. Let's not go through this again."

"Baby, please. We don't have a whole lot of time, let's just do it."

"No." He had already managed to unhook my bra and unbutton my jeans. His hands were all over me. And as long as we didn't go too far, it felt wonderful. But the more I tried to resist, the more insistent he became.

"Damn it, Whitney. What the hell is wrong with you? I thought you loved me. I thought you wanted to be with me. I've given you everything. I call you every day. I walk you to class. I quit basketball for you. I skipped class to come and see you. Everybody hates me because of you. What else do you want from me? All I want is to be with you and to spend some time with you. Is that too much to ask?"

"Kevin, I don't want us to start fighting again. I just don't want to do this. You know I love you, and I love spending time with you. But the doctor said that if I get pregnant again, I could die. If you really cared about me, you'd understand!"

"What, you think I don't care about you? You know that's not true. I'd do anything for you. I just want to be with you." He reached in the pocket of his pants and pulled out a couple of condoms.

"See, I even brought protection to show you how much I care about you. I just want to be with you." I begged and pleaded with him the whole time to stop, but he didn't. He pinned me down in the back of the car and ripped the buttons off my shirt. This wasn't the guy I had fallen in love with. He seemed like some crazed maniac who was obsessed with having sex—no matter what I said or did.

I tried to push him away, which only made things worse. I tried to sit up, but my hair was pinned under his hands, and his weight was too much for me to resist. Kevin kissed me so hard my teeth cut into my bottom lip, making it bleed. He grabbed the waist of my jeans and pulled them down to my ankles along with my panties, and forced himself inside of me. "You know you want this," he said. "Girl, I love you so much. That's why I want us to be together."

Kevin told me how much he loved me the entire time he was raping me.

He used two condoms, and they both came off inside of me. The moment he finished, I knew I was pregnant again. And I was right. The doctor had given me a death sentence if I got pregnant again. I wasn't sure if I'd live to see my 16th birthday.

For the most part, Kevin and I fought and had sex. Despite the risks that the doctor had shared with us,

Kevin didn't seem to care. Every conversation we had always ended in us talking about sex and eventually having sex. This was not the kind, sweet guy who I used to know. And I wasn't the same innocent little girl I used to be either.

Between classes, we started having sex in the open stairwell at school. We even skipped lunch to have sex. I was always scared we were going to get caught. Occasionally, we would sneak off to the vocational building that was no longer in use for a 10-minute "quickie."

Sex consumed our relationship. It wasn't even enjoyable anymore. It always started with a fight and ended with me crying from the pain or from the humiliation. Kevin started saying things like, "After all I've done for you and given up for you, this is the least you can do. You owe me this much." Surprisingly enough, I believed him.

After a while, we stopped using protection. Kevin reasoned that if I was already pregnant, then I couldn't get pregnant again. I was too afraid to tell anyone that I might be pregnant, so I didn't say anything at all. The doctor's words echoed in the back of my mind. Honestly, I was afraid to know the truth; because the reality was that I could die from getting pregnant again. I wasn't ready to face that.

Things were very tense around my house. Kevin and I weren't getting along, so that made me hard to deal with. My mom and stepdad were arguing more too. Ever since she allowed me to continue to see Kevin against his wishes, things had been going downhill between them. My stepfather was spending increasing amounts of time away from the house without explanation. At first it didn't seem to bother my mom. She had another boyfriend anyway, but nobody was supposed to know. I always knew.

I waited until I was almost four months pregnant before telling my mom. I weighed my options and finally decided that I was more afraid of dying than her being

mad that I was pregnant again. I convinced myself that my mom would be more concerned with the potential consequences than with me making the same mistake twice. So I broke down and told her.

We went back to the same doctor that had seen me before. The nurse gave me a pregnancy test and informed my mom and me that I was four months pregnant. When the physician came in and saw I had returned again, he refused to treat me or to perform the abortion. We figured he didn't want to be bothered with another hardheaded teenager who had ignored his advice. But in fact, it was a complicated procedure that he didn't want to be liable for if something went wrong.

We looked in the telephone directory and found a high-risk pregnancy clinic. We drove an hour to the city, and at age 15, I had my second abortion. My parents were very supportive. Kevin wasn't there this time.

Sometimes life is stranger than fiction. When my parents and I walked out of the abortion clinic, there were police cars and a fire engine in the parking lot surrounding my stepdad's brand new car. For no obvious reason, the car had caught on fire and was engulfed in flames by the time the authorities arrived. There was no sign of foul play, a hate crime, or anything else within reason. It was just one of those things that happened for no other reason than to make us think about where our lives were heading. My stepdad loved that car—and now it had been destroyed. Who knows… maybe it was a sign from God.

Once again, Kevin's parents helped my parents with the doctor bill. Surprisingly, they forgave us again. But this time they said, "just don't let it happen again." Even after this pregnancy, I still didn't get on the pill. I guess my mother figured with me having to go through what I had experienced, sex would be the furthest thing from my mind. Our parents were getting the picture and realized we were going to be together no matter what.

Now with Kevin and I conceiving and loosing yet another baby, I thought my days of convincing him that I loved him (and only him) were over, but he became more jealous and controlling than ever. Our relationship was back in the honeymoon phase, but the calm before the next storm wouldn't last long.

One morning at school, Kevin and I got into a fight in the hallway. He accused me of not loving him and of seeing someone else. I denied it, and he shoved me into a locker and walked away. I went to my chemistry class and stared at the blackboard with tears streaming down my face.

My lab partner was a nice guy named Chris. He was popular, athletic and good-looking. He had asked me out once before I started dating Kevin. Chris helped me make it through class by sharing his notes and letting me review the previous night's homework, which I hadn't done. The bell rang and Chris walked out of class with his arm around my shoulder. He whispered in my ear that everything was going to be OK, squeezed my hand, and left for his next class. I waved goodbye and turned around to see Kevin staring me dead in my eyes.

I never got a chance to explain. "Who was that? I knew you were seeing somebody else. How could you do this to me, Whitney," he practically yelled. Two teachers noticed us, and Kevin loosened the grip he had on my arm and lowered his voice.

"Kevin, I can't talk to you when you're acting like this. That guy was just my chemistry lab partner. There's nothing between us—I hardly know him. He was just helping me with my homework. I love you! Don't you believe me?" We approached the stairwell and I turned around to face him. "Look, I've got to get to my next class," I said. The hall hadn't quite cleared out as the final bell for class rang. "Come on Kevin, don't start this again. There's nobody but you. I love you, and I want to be with you forever."

I turned to say goodbye and head down the stairs. Kevin pinned me up against the wall and started kissing me roughly. "You belong to me, and you're going to do exactly what I tell you to do," he said. I pushed him away from me, and he grabbed me; he twisted my arm and shoved me down the flight of stairs. My books spilled all over the floor, and the fall knocked the wind out of me.

"Look what you made me do," Kevin said, looking over me as I lay sprawled on the floor at the bottom of the stairs. All I could do was cry. But I still loved him.

There were lots of witnesses to what Kevin had done to me, and we all knew he was in trouble. The principal called both Kevin's mom and my mom up to the school. He was determined to put an end to the abuse in school.

As I was sitting in his office waiting for my mom, I heard a lot of commotion outside and a voice that sounded a lot like my grandmother. I was right. It was my grandmother, and she was mad.

We jumped up to see what was happening and realized that my grandmother had run into Kevin as she was coming into the office, grabbed him by the collar and pinned him up against a locker. She snarled at him, "If you put your hands on my granddaughter again, I will kill you. Do you understand me?" Her words were loud, slow and deliberate. Kevin was at least a foot taller and a hundred pounds heavier than she was, but he dared not retaliate against her. He knew my grandmother was serious. In spite of the severity of the situation, it was a hilarious sight. It happened right as we were changing classes and all the kids saw Kevin being assaulted by my grandmother.

The kids teased him for months about that day; and he never lived it down.

To everyone around me, Kevin was showing the classic signs of becoming a chronic abuser. He was jealous and controlling, and he didn't have a problem lying to someone's face. And most importantly, he had hit me.

For me, these were just a few isolated incidents. Kevin was simply misunderstood. Nobody knew the sweet, loving, Prince Charming that I had fallen in love with. Plus, the fight was my fault anyway—I had provoked him. This was between Kevin and me, and we would work things out.

The hallways at school were crowded as usual on Monday morning, but this day there was a buzz in the air and a lot of strange, questioning and sympathetic glances being shot at me. Girls I didn't know whispered behind my back and stole quick looks over their shoulders before shaking their heads in disapproval.

Obviously, the word had gotten out about what was going on between Kevin and me. I didn't care what anyone else thought. I knew the real truth about my relationship with Kevin, and I didn't need anyone else's approval. Even my bus driver pulled me aside and begged me to leave him alone. She never seemed to like me before, but on this day, she actually seemed to care.

My female cousins practically chased me down in the hallways between classes all day. Everybody wanted to hear the story over and over again in explicit detail. And everybody had a lot of bad advice to offer me.

My cousin Tina ran up behind me and practically put me in a chokehold. "Whitney, what in the world did he do to you," she screamed in my ear.

"Shhhh…" I motioned to her to lower her voice before I'd spill my guts. We had about three and a half minutes before the next bell for class rang, but I told Tina and my friends Angela and Faith who had caught up with us in the hall the whole story.

"You guys, it was no big deal," I said. "We just got into an argument and he made a mistake. It was my fault. Kevin saw me talking to another guy. He wanted us to spend some more time together, and I acted like I didn't want to be with him. He just thought I didn't love him anymore. The argument just got a little out of control and…"

"And he hit you, girl," Angela said angrily. "And then he pushed you down a flight of stairs."

"No, it wasn't like that," I pleaded with them; hoping they wouldn't make this a bigger deal than it was.

"So, what was it like, Whitney? What's going on with you two," Faith asked. "A few weeks ago, my mom said that she heard from my aunt that your mother could still see his handprint on your face when you got back to the house. That doesn't sound like an accident to me. Girl, you don't have to put up with that kind of crap. And now this? You should drop him and get out while you still can. Are you listening to me? Look, I've got to get to class. Angela, Tina, tell your friend here that she needs to drop this fool.

"He's not that fine, and there are plenty of other guys who would love to ask her out—and they're not afraid of Kevin either. They all know he's a punk. Yeah, he doesn't have a problem hitting a girl, but the guys on the basketball team said he's a punk when it comes to fighting another guy. Whitney, I gotta run, but I'll call you later tonight."

Faith looked over her shoulder and mouthed the words "drop him" as she headed off to class. I just waved at her and let the words fall on deaf ears.

The whole morning was quite eventful. All my thoughts focused on Kevin and what had happened between us. This wasn't the guy I had fallen in love with. I convinced myself that whatever was wrong, our love would fix. I honestly believed that Kevin would never hit me again.

I hardly got a chance to talk with Kevin alone on Monday because all his coaches and former teammates had formed a protective guard around him to find out what was going on. I heard rumors all day from my girlfriends that they were trying to find out if he had really hit me and shoved me down the stairs, or if I had made it up. In between trying to convince him to play basketball again and prevent him from ruining his life with me, they attempted to advise him on the appropriate ways that a guy should treat his girlfriend. Their words fell on deaf ears too.

"Hey Kevin, man let's go shoot some hoops in the gym during lunch," his friend Mike said. "We've heard all kinds of crazy stuff about what happened between you and Whitney. Yo man, what's going on? Just meet us in the gym, OK?" Kevin hunched his shoulders and walked down the hall to his classroom just as the bell was ringing. In his mind, nothing was wrong, and there was nothing else to talk about.

Kevin tried to avoid his classmates, but they tracked him down anyway.

His friend Mike started it, "Hey man, there's some crazy stuff going around in school about you. What's up with you and Whitney? Folks are making it seem like you beat her down. What happened?"

"Man, it wasn't like that. Nothing happened," Kevin said.

"Come on Kevin, I heard that you punched her and almost broke her jaw," said Greg. "People were talking about it in school and after church on Sunday. They were talking about having you arrested and sent to jail for assaulting a female."

Kevin just looked at him and rolled his eyes. "Greg, you've known me since we were four years old. You know that's not true. Give me some kind of credit. I have never hit a female before, and I'll never hit a female. Just leave me alone," Kevin said.

"Hey, I'm on your side," Mike said. "Just be careful. Don't let this thing get out of hand. Whitney's a nice girl, and you two have got a good thing going. Maybe y'all should just chill out a little bit—let things die down and then get back together."

Kevin shook his head and said, "I told you, everything's fine, so just drop it. Whitney and me are going to work through this together, and we don't need a whole bunch of people in our business. I don't want to talk about this anymore. Let's just shoot some hoops before class starts."

Students at school were constantly talking about us. Soon we were the talk around both of our towns. People thought our lives were better than the daytime soap operas. They began to refer to us as the 'fighting couple.' Everybody knew that something was vastly wrong with our relationship. But, I kept my head held high, because I hadn't done anything wrong.

My main priority was trying to keep my relationship with Kevin intact. Honestly, I felt it was my job to protect him, because nobody else understood him.

Between our episodes of fighting and sex, he would continue to send me cards, candy and flowers to make up for it. He was starting to do all the things his own father did to excuse his abusive behavior. Somehow money, gifts and apologies were supposed to make up for abuse and rape.

Our perfect relationship was gone and had been replaced by something horrible. But I still justified his behavior and made excuses for the way he treated me. I convinced myself—and those around me—that Kevin was under a lot of pressure, but underneath he was still a good guy. I knew that things between us would be OK. I wanted to believe that. I needed to believe that.

The end of the school year was a couple of weeks away. Our parents figured that the three months of vacation apart would do us some good. They wouldn't have to worry about me getting pregnant again or Kevin and me fighting. Even I thought that time apart would be the best thing for us, but it wasn't long before Mr. Charming came back and convinced me once again that he had changed.

Before long I was back to manipulating my mom into letting us see each other again. This time it didn't go as planned, and she didn't give in as quickly as Kevin and I would have liked. So Kevin put his clever mind into action and decided to come up with another plan. Nothing was going to keep us apart.

The greatest tragedy about being in an abusive relationship is no longer being able to decipher the reality of the situation. Facts and fiction get intermingled, and it's hard to tell the truth from a lie. I knew Kevin had slapped me out of anger—but it was the first time. I thought it would be the only time.

That wasn't really abuse, I reasoned. Being grabbed and pushed down the stairs was more difficult to justify. He said he was sorry and would never do it again, but then he lied about it to the authorities, his parents and mine. If it was really a mistake, shouldn't he have just owned up to it and then tried to make things better? I was starting to get confused. I knew something wasn't right, but I was so blinded by love, I just couldn't see it.

Chapter 3: "Profile of an Abuser"

"Now ladies, I've told you part of my story. Now, I want to hear your stories," Whitney said. You don't have to tell the group everything, but this is where the healing process begins. You've been in pain long enough; you've been a victim long enough. In here, we are survivors!"

There were eight women in the room. Tonight, instead of bumps and bruises, they were wearing emotional badges of courage. They had finally escaped and gotten away from the hell of domestic violence and abuse in their marriages and relationships.

The women were from various stations in life. They were young and old. They were business class and working class. Some were educated and some were not. The group of women didn't represent any particular race or ethnicity. It was obvious that domestic violence and abusive relationships didn't discriminate.

"Now, who wants to go first," Whitney asked. "Remember that everything said in here stays in here. It's not just about privacy and respect—somebody's life may be on the line. So, before we go any further, just take about five minutes and tell us your name, how long you were a victim and when you became a survivor."

Whitney walked to the corner of the room and placed an easel filled with terms and definitions in front of the group, then took a seat in the circle amongst the other women.

Domestic Violence—Domestic violence is defined as abuse from a current or former intimate partner: ex/boyfriend, ex/husband, ex/girlfriend, ex/wife. Domestic violence can mean physical abuse—pushing, slapping, hitting or choking; but it also can include: emotional abuse, threats, intimidation, isolation, sexual abuse, and economic abuse, using the children or using "male privilege." (Male privilege is defined as controlling behavior where masculinity is used as a weapon to define gender roles and to mistreat a woman into submission. Ex. He is the "king of the castle," and she is his servant.)

Sexual Assault—Sexual assault is any unwanted sexual contact or attention achieved by force, threats, bribes, manipulation, pressure, tricks or violence. Sexual assault may be physical or non-physical and includes rape and attempted rape, child molestation, incest and sexual harassment.

Rape—Rape is forcible sexual penetration (vaginal, oral or anal) against a person who has not consented. Rape is a criminal act that can be committed by a stranger, acquaintance, spouse, relative or co-worker. (Interact)

*THE CRIMES OF DOMESTIC VIOLENCE, SEXUAL ASSAULT AND RAPE ARE ALL PUNISHABLE BY LAW!

Karen raised her hand and said, "I know I already introduced myself, but I also wanted to introduce my daughter, Deborah, to the group. She came here with me tonight for moral support. She observed what I went through, and now that she's dating, I just wanted her to learn more about some of the warning signs of an abuser."

"Oh, that's easy," Nancy said. "Selfish. Arrogant. Jealous."

"Don't forget insecure," Yolanda chimed in.

"And critical. My ex-boyfriend was extremely mean-spirited and critical of everything I did," Diana said. "He was obsessive, and nothing ever satisfied him. Nothing and no one—including me—was ever good enough for him. He was charming at first, but then he just had to criticize everything: my hair, my clothes, my car, my menu selection, and my make-up. He became so obnoxious, it was unbearable."

Whitney said, "Deborah, there are a lot of warning signs of an abuser, but not all of them act the same way. Also, there are different types of abuse. And that's a good place for us to begin our discussion tonight as we get to know each other. Can anyone else name some of the different types of abuse?"

Pattie raised her hand. "Physical, sexual, mental, emotional and financial."

"Don't forget verbal abuse," Karen said.

"Very good," Whitney said. "Let me repeat those for everyone. There are several types of abuse, but all of them are damaging and hurtful. There's physical, sexual, mental, emotional, financial and verbal abuse. Can anyone share an example of their experiences in any of those areas?"

Deborah raised her hand and said, "This happened to my aunt—my mom's sister. For years, she was the victim of financial and emotional abuse. Even though her husband never put his hands on her, he slowly destroyed her with his cruelty and controlling attitude.

"My aunt graduated from college and had a successful career as an artist before she got married. Then when she met her husband, he told her that 'no woman of his was going to work.' So, she gave up her dreams of painting and sculpting to make him happy. But that also made her completely dependent on his paycheck.

"At first it was OK, because he made enough money to provide for them. But when the company he worked for went out of business, he had to take a lesser-paying job at another company, and he blamed their financial hardship on my aunt. He always told her that she spent too much money and that they wouldn't be in such bad shape if it wasn't for her.

"When my aunt volunteered to go back to work, he ridiculed her and said that she wasn't talented enough to make a living as an artist. He took away her credit cards and made her close her bank account. He took control of all the money and even put her on an allowance.

"He started opening her mail to make sure she wasn't hiding money from him. He wouldn't allow her to buy new clothes or shoes, even when the ones she was wearing became worn.

"Then he started going with her to the grocery store to make sure she didn't spend too much. I remember once, my cousin sent her some money to help out with personal items, and my aunt's husband took that away too. It just got ridiculous. She finally left him, but he convinced her to come back, and the cycle started all over again."

Whitney said, "That's an excellent example. Even though he didn't punch or hit her, he still managed to damage her self-esteem and take financial control over her life. OK, does anyone else have other examples?"

Nancy slowly raised her hand. "My first husband was extremely jealous, and before it was all over, he began stalking me. I slept with a knife under the covers every night—afraid that he was going to try and kill me. When I left for work in the mornings, he would follow me to see if I was secretly meeting with another man. He would open my mail, come to my job and go through my closet. I don't really know what he was looking for.

"I was always faithful to him, but he never believed me. The more insecure he became, the more scared I became."

Nancy's voice was trembling as she spoke and she was nervously twiddling her thumbs while she spoke. Whitney spoke up, "It's OK, Nancy. Take your time. You're a survivor and you made it out. We're here to support you—just take your time."

Nancy continued, "One day I came home from work early. It had been a very stressful week at the office, and I had a migraine. My boss gave me the afternoon off, so I went home. I decided to take a warm shower and go to bed early. When I stepped out of the shower, my husband suddenly appeared from behind me, grabbed me around my neck and held a knife to my throat. He accused me of cheating on him just because I was taking a shower in the middle of the afternoon.

"He started calling my friends and even some of my co-workers to see if they knew whether I was seeing someone else. The whole situation was just absurd. I'm so glad we never had children together, because I wouldn't have been able to sleep at night knowing that my kids were in the same house with him."

"So how did the situation end," Whitney asked.

"Ironically enough," Nancy said, "I found out he had never divorced his first wife. He had another family in a nearby city. Can you believe that? All that time, he was accusing me of being unfaithful, and he had another wife and family that he was taking care of. I filed for an annulment and took out a restraining order against him. I still don't sleep very well at night, but I'm just taking it one day at the time." Deborah was sitting beside Nancy and leaned over and gave her a hug.

Yolanda slowly cleared her throat and started to speak. Toni—who was sitting beside her—gave her a pat on the shoulder for encouragement.

"My name is Yolanda, and I'm a survivor of domestic violence. My late ex-husband raped me, beat me, and then attempted to kill me and both of our two small children.

"We were married a total of 13 years, and our marriage started off like a fairy tale. It was the most beautiful wedding you can imagine—it was everything I dreamed of. Everyone thought he was the perfect husband. He was good-looking, charming, intelligent and successful.

"He was so loving and attentive, I thought I would have a perfect life with him." A tear rolled down Yolanda's cheek, and her voice got caught in her throat when she tried to speak. All eyes in the room were on Yolanda as she gathered her composure and continued to share her story.

"My husband was a big-wig in the corporate world. And the more promotions he got and the more money he made, the more stressed out he became. He started drinking. It began as social drinking and then he started drinking more at home. He started hiding alcohol throughout the house and in our bedroom closet. He would work hard all week, then drink to drown his stress and sorrows on the weekend. When I tried to talk to him, it only turned into an argument.

"Then the arguing escalated into fighting. I would get depressed on Fridays because I knew that we were going to be fighting all weekend.

"What I hated the most was how he still pretended to be 'Mr. Wonderful' in public and in front of our friends. Do you know that he sang in the church choir every Sunday and sat on the deacon board at our church?

When I went to talk with our pastor, he told me that I was over-exaggerating and that any other woman would be grateful to have such a kind and caring husband like Ted.

"One Sunday afternoon, we came home from church, and Ted went straight to the kitchen cabinet and took out a bottle of hard liquor. I told him that I didn't like how much he was drinking, and that I thought we should go to counseling. He called me the "b-word," slapped me and punched me in the stomach. He told me that I was ungrateful and that I was lucky that he wanted me— because no other man would put up with such an ugly, dumb and ungrateful tramp like me."

The tears streamed down Yolanda's face. Whitney took out a tissue from a small box under her chair and handed it to Yolanda. Then she passed the box around because there wasn't a dry eye in the room.

Yolanda sniffed, wiped her eyes and continued. "I tried to convince myself that things were going to get better. After all, this was the man I loved. We decided to start a family, and I prayed that things would improve once we had kids.

"They didn't. I went into premature labor and delivered my oldest child three weeks early because Ted hit me in the stomach while he was drunk. He just didn't care about anything or anybody but himself. That same cycle continued for years. He would pretend to be the perfect husband, father, employee, provider and Christian all week, and then he would turn into somebody I didn't even recognize on Friday and Saturday nights."

Yolanda leaned over and rolled up her pant leg. "This scar is from where he threw a ceramic vase at me. I had to get 14 stitches to close the wound." Then she rolled up her right sleeve. "He broke my arm in two places—I can hardly use it anymore. And one night, during one of his drinking binges, he grabbed me by my neck and tried to strangle me. I woke up in the hospital with an I.V. in my arm." Yolanda stopped speaking, and the color drained from her face.

"It's OK Yolanda," Whitney said. "We're here for you."

"I – I – I… can't. It hurts too much. My life is over, and my children don't have a father anymore, and it's all my fault."

Whitney asked, "Yolanda, do you mind if I tell the group the end of your story?" By now, Yolanda was shaking with emotion and several of the other women tried to console her. She slowly nodded her head "OK."

"Ladies, in Yolanda's case it was either kill or be killed. Yolanda was acquitted of charges for killing her husband. The court ruled it was self-defense, and she was allowed to keep her two children. Why don't we all take a 10-minute break?"

When the women came back in the room, Whitney had put up another chart with some statistics about domestic violence:

• IN 93% OF THE REPORTED DOMESTIC VIOLENCE CASES, FEMALES ARE THE VICTIMS, AND MALES ARE THE PERPETRATORS—THE OTHER 7% ARE MALE VICTIMS IN EITHER A HOMOSEXUAL MALE RELATIONSHIP OR RELATIONSHIP WITH A FEMALE PERPETRATOR

• AN ESTIMATED FOUR MILLION AMERICAN WOMEN ARE ABUSED EACH YEAR BY THEIR HUSBANDS OR PARTNERS

• VIOLENCE OCCURS AT LEAST ONCE IN TWO-THIRDS OF ALL MARRIAGES

- MANY WOMEN ARE BATTERED PHYSICALLY FOR THE FIRST TIME DURING PREGNANCY OR ON THEIR HONEYMOON NIGHT

- 50% OF ALL HOMELESS WOMEN AND CHILDREN IN THE UNITED STATES ARE FLEEING DOMESTIC ABUSE

- 85% OF ABUSERS LEARNED THEIR ABUSIVE HABITS AT HOME

- 50% OF MEN ARRESTED ARE ALSO SEXUALLY OR PHYSICALLY ABUSING OTHER FAMILY MEMBERS

- CHILDREN WHO WITNESS DOMESTIC VIOLENCE ARE FOUR (4) TIMES MORE LIKELY TO BE ARRESTED BY THE POLICE THAN CHILDREN WHO DON'T WITNESS DOMESTIC VIOLENCE

- 63% OF CHILDREN IN JAIL FOR MURDER ARE THERE FOR KILLING AN ABUSIVE PARENT

- 80% OF JUVENILE RUNAWAYS COME FROM VIOLENT HOMES

- CHILDREN WHO WITNESS DOMESTIC VIOLENCE ARE SIX (6) TIMES MORE LIKELY TO COMMIT SUICIDE

• 98% OF DOMESTIC VIOLENCE VICTIMS ARE MISDIAGNOSED IN AN EMERGENCY ROOM

• 75% OF WOMEN KILLED EACH YEAR IN DOMESTIC VIOLENCE DIE AFTER THEY LEAVE THEIR ABUSER

• ONLY 50% OF THE VICTIMS OF DOMESTIC VIOLENCE REPORT THE INCIDENTS TO THE POLICE

(Information extracted from the Bureau of Justice Statistics & Interact)

"Before we leave tonight," Whitney said, "I want each of you to think about your life and the life of a young woman you love and care about. Domestic violence can end those lives prematurely. Tonight, we are putting a stop to violence in our lives and taking a stand to protect ourselves and our families." She handed out some pamphlets to each of the women and instructed them to read the material and be prepared to create a new life plan for starting over the following week.

Whitney told the group, "As you leave, be sure to share an encouraging word with at least one of the women you met here tonight. It's always good to make new friends that you can trust—and who understand your particular situation."

As the others left the room, Karen and her daughter Deborah stayed behind. "Whitney, I know it's been a long day and you're probably ready to go home, but I'd really like to hear more about your story," Karen said. "I've lived through this nightmare, and I just don't want my daughter to have to endure the kind of torture that I did. Would you mind sharing some more details about your personal story with us? I'm really interested in knowing if your ex-husband had any type of personality disorders or other signs that contributed to his behavior."

Whitney gestured for the two women to take a seat. "I don't mind sharing at all. This is what I've dedicated my life's work to doing. In my case, Kevin was eventually diagnosed with Obsessive Compulsive

Disorder and Bipolar Disorder. Once in jail, he underwent a psychiatric evaluation, and there were also indications of a Paranoid Personality Disorder with narcissistic and obsessive/compulsive features.

"According to the results of his test, Kevin demonstrated an exaggerated and superior sense of self worth and an abrasive social manner. That explains why he had so few friends when we were in high school— and why he couldn't hold down a job for very long. Overall, the report said that he had a habitual and maladaptive method of relating, behaving, thinking and feeling.

"I know that's a lot of psychobabble, but what it really means is that Kevin acted as if he owned the world, and everybody in it owed him something. He had severe mood swings that made him come across like Dr. Jekyll and Mr. Hyde.

"Some days, I wouldn't know which personality to expect because his moods changed so rapidly. You may have also heard bi-polar disorders referred to as 'manic-depressive disorders,' and they cause an individual to have extreme mood changes that affect social interaction and decision-making processes and impulsive or reckless behavior. Kevin would just snap and do things without thinking. You just never knew what was going to come next."

Deborah asked, "What symptoms showed up with the paranoid personality disorder?" Whitney shook her head in disgust as she recalled the memories from her relationship.

She said, "Kevin and I got into a million arguments because he constantly accused me of seeing someone else or sleeping with someone else. One of the most telling signs of a paranoia disorder is suspicion and an overactive imagination. People with that disorder tend to think that others are trying to harm them, and they find it very difficult to trust people—even those they love. Kevin always felt like it was 'him against the world'— and that everybody was out to get him.

"Even when he went to jail, his psychological evaluation states that he was complaining about how unfairly he was being treated, and how the 'system' only worked for people with power or money. He never thought to mention his wrongdoing or his criminal behavior, and how he had destroyed our family."

Whitney continued to explain how Kevin's fits of jealous rage and controlling attitude had damaged her self-esteem in high school and escalated into violence. Her words were filled with emotion, as if she was reliving each moment of the abuse as she spoke.

"That summer, Kevin's attitude began to change right before my very eyes. With each passing month, his moves got bolder and bolder. Kevin wasn't going to spend the entire summer without seeing me, so he began to sneak over to my house in the middle of the night.

"He began to manipulate and control my life, and he started using sex as a weapon against me. He would park his car at a local convenience store near my house, wait until the house was dark and my parents were asleep, and sneak into my window at night.

"There was a large walk-in closet in my bedroom. That's where Kevin and I spent most of our time together at night. I knew that what we were doing was wrong, but I didn't let that stop me. Kevin started treating me like his own personal servant. Before he would arrive, I had to cook dinner for him and then have sex in the closet— while my parents slept on the other side of the house."

Deborah looked at her with disbelief. "Weren't you afraid that your parents would catch you," she asked. Whitney nodded her head and answered, "That was always a concern, but honestly, I was more afraid of what Kevin would do to me if I didn't go along with him than whatever punishment my parents would give me."

Whitney explained how each day she found herself spending more and more time having to defend herself and deny the accusations that Kevin was making against her. He started dictating her schedule, wardrobe, social activities, friends and every move. And after he had controlled her all day at school, he would call her in the evenings, and they spent countless more hours talking on the phone. It became a predictable cycle that started and repeated again each morning. At night after her parents had gone to bed, he would sneak over, she would cook for him, have sex with him, and then he would hit her as a reminder of who was in control; then he left.

"Suicidal thoughts became common during our relationship," Whitney said. "One night, I even threatened to kill myself with a pair of scissors. I needed Kevin to understand how much I loved him, but no matter what I said, it didn't seem to make a difference.

"The man I once considered to be my best friend was now turning into my worst enemy. He used my fears, weaknesses and insecurities against me. Our relationship and communication reeked of fear and intimidation."

Whitney emphasized to Deborah and her mother that jealous rage, angry outbursts, manipulation and control were not loving characteristics of a healthy relationship. "Those were the most obvious signs," Whitney said. "If I had known then what I know now, I would have run away from him. But of course, only hindsight has 20-20 vision."

Karen said, "I'm not sure I understand how you could be a teenager living in the same house with your parents and they not know something was wrong. That just doesn't make sense to me. My daughter and I have always been very close, and I always encouraged her to talk openly with me and tell me anything that was on her mind. Did your parents ever realize what was going on or do anything to intervene?"

Whitney explained how she never made Kevin out to be the bad guy. Even as the severity of the situation began to escalate, she always took his side. She hid everything from her parents, and Kevin's behavior became even more erratic.

Whitney continued, "One night in particular, he came over to see me too early—before my parents had gone to bed. My mother was in my room talking to me and happened to look up and see Kevin outside my window. She immediately ran to the window and started yelling at him. 'Kevin, get over here!' The sound of my mother's voice startled him.

"He darted across the yard, and ran to his car, which had been parked behind the local store. That incident was the first time both of our parents decided that enough was enough and intervened."

Whitney remembered the incident and told the two women how her parents had finally contacted the police about Kevin.

She recalled the day they went to court. Kevin sat in front of the judge looking dejected and despondent.

Whitney's parents had accused him of trespassing and pressed charges against him. His own father had scolded, grounded and threatened him. The night that Whitney's mother saw him outside the bedroom window, she immediately called his parents and told them what was going on. Kevin's father had vowed to end the relationship one way or the other.

The incident leading up to his court appearance had happened a few months earlier. When Kevin got home from Whitney's house, his father slowly walked into his bedroom and closed the door. He spoke in a very even tone and warned his son about becoming too serious in a relationship too early. His calm demeanor quickly escalated into fury. In no uncertain terms, he expressed how disappointed they were that Kevin had become obsessed with Whitney, and how they felt the relationship was destroying his chances for a successful future.

Then, Kevin's father reached under his shirt and pulled out a gun. He grabbed Kevin by the neck, held the gun to the side of his head and said very slowly, "We're not going to put up with this any longer. If you don't get your life together, I'm going to end it for you. If you pull another stunt like this one, I'm going to blow your head off. Do you understand me?"

Kevin was shaking and practically passed out from fear. He tried to maintain his composure and answer, but the words got stuck in his throat. His whole body was trembling, and a cold sweat broke out on his forehead. He knew that his father was serious. He had seen his dad's violent tendencies toward his mother—and wasn't sure whether or not his dad was going to pull the trigger. And even if he didn't pull the trigger this time, you never knew when he was going to lose control and fly off the handle. This was a life-changing moment for Kevin.

Meanwhile, the tension in the Jordan family household was thick enough to slice. Whitney's mom had done some further investigation with the convenience store owner and several neighbors—and learned that Kevin had been parking there at night for quite some time. They had more than enough evidence and witnesses to prove that Kevin had been trespassing. Whitney's mom confronted her about her relationship with Kevin and what had been going on at night. Every conversation turned into an argument about trust, disappointment, irresponsible behavior, etc.

Since Whitney and Kevin couldn't figure out how to separate on their own, her parents decided to let the local police help them expedite the process. The very next morning, Whitney's mom went down to the police station and pressed charges.

Whitney relived the entire experience in her mind and then shared it with the two women: "Kevin's court date was coming up in a couple of months. In addition to the break up of our relationship by both of our parents, my parents had it in for me. I had all phone privileges taken away. When they left home, they would take the phones with them to make sure I didn't contact Kevin. I could only go to school and to my part-time job; no more extracurricular activities. My parents had lost so much trust in me that I could no longer sleep with my bedroom door closed. But to me, my parents' punishment was a piece of cake compared to what I had to go through with Kevin.

"Every day leading up to the court date he pressured me to convince my parents to drop the charges against him. He began making me skip lunch and meet him in the vocational building so he could interrogate me. Kevin constantly told me the situation was all my fault, and that it was my obligation to get him off the hook. I believed him. I would go home and try talking to my mom about dropping the charges, but she wouldn't budge. Every time I came back and told him the charges weren't getting dropped he would beat me up in school and then force me to have sex.

"The more Kevin and I fought, the more withdrawn I became. I still loved him with all my heart, but he only seemed interested in getting himself out of trouble. By now, he was forcing me to secretly have sex with him at school every day. I was now having sex with Kevin out of obligation—not because I loved him. I was too scared to tell anyone what was going on, and I was too afraid to confront him for fear that he was going to hit me again. I felt my loyalty was to Kevin instead of myself.

"Stress and anxiety ruled my life. I was dealing with tension at home between my parents, and tension at school with Kevin. Every relationship in my life was strained.

"I had tried and failed to get the charges dropped up until the night before his court date. Kevin finally decided to take matters into his own hands and showed up at my house to speak to my parents himself. As we sat on the couch, Kevin did what he did best—and talked his way out of trouble. He apologized, begged and pleaded with my parents to help him. He vowed never to defy them again and assured them that he had learned his lesson."

Scenes from that night flashed through Kevin's mind as he sat in the courtroom awaiting his sentence for the trespassing charges. Whitney's parents didn't drop the charges but said they would speak on Kevin's behalf in court. They were determined to teach him a lesson and make him accept responsibility for his actions. Kevin and Whitney just sat quietly in the courtroom as the judge issued him a reduced sentence of community service; picking up trash and cleaning up the neighborhood.

Picking up trash on Saturday mornings for the next couple of months was beneath Kevin. He felt like a second-class citizen and he wasn't happy at all.

Kevin watched his life deteriorating one layer at a time. He now had a juvenile criminal record, Whitney's parents despised him, and his own father had threatened to kill him. Adding insult to injury, he was cut from the basketball team—even though he was their star player and had vowed to return and help them have a winning season. The team cut him out of spite.

Whitney leaned in closely as she talked to Karen and Deborah in the L.I.P.S. meeting room. She wanted them both to understand and learn from her experiences. She had their full attention.

She continued, "the old saying is true that the more things change, the more they stay the same. By my senior year in high school, as a result of my sexual obligation to Kevin, I was now pregnant for the third time. I considered keeping this one.

"My mother called Kevin's mother from the clinic on the day of my appointment. I stood beside her quietly listening to the conversation. I felt sick."

'Hello? Mrs. Little? Yes, this is Mrs. Jordan—Whitney's mother. I think we both know that this entire situation has gotten out of hand. We're here at the doctor's office, and this is Whitney's third pregnancy. We're thinking about keeping the baby this time, and I was just calling to let you and your husband know.'

"Kevin's mother almost choked on her words, 'Oh no, you can't do that! You've got to put an end to this.

Kevin is leaving for college this year. He's got his whole future ahead of him. No son of mine is going to drop out of school and start working somewhere earning minimum wage. These kids can't afford to take care of a baby. They aren't responsible enough to take care of a child. You cannot let her do this. You've got to put a stop to this now!'

"Kevin's mother never even asked how I was doing. His parents hated me at this point. And they weren't too pleased with him either, but he was still their pride and joy; I, on the other hand, was expendable.

"Once again, Kevin had charmed, lied and manipulated the situation to his advantage. Since things weren't going his way, he decided to punish me instead. For a short period of time, I was no longer his girlfriend—just an occasional good time and sexual release whenever he got the urge. He controlled me with fear and force. And even though he was still having sex with me, he started dating someone else. When I told Kevin that I was pregnant for the third time, he denied that it was his—even though he was still the only guy I had ever been intimate with.

"Kevin also convinced his parents that the baby wasn't his since we were no longer a couple. He even invited another girl to come over to prove his case. Of course, they believed him.

"I could tell by my mother's expression that Mrs. Little had said something to enrage her. 'What do you mean the baby isn't his,' she practically yelled into the phone. 'Who else could it belong to? Whitney spends

every waking minute with your son, and I know for a fact that she's in love with him, so I know this baby is his—just like the other two.'

"Kevin's mother was talking so loudly at this point, that I could hear her from several feet away. 'Kevin and Whitney aren't even dating anymore. My son is headed to college, and I'm not going to let Whitney trap him and pin this pregnancy on him. He's got a bright future ahead of him, and I'm not going to let her ruin it!'

"For all intents and purposes, the conversation was over. Mrs. Little was still talking, but my mother just quietly hung up the phone.

"The nurse walked out and escorted us into one of the examination rooms. For the first time ever, I saw my baby on the ultrasound. It finally became real to me that this was a child—a life that Kevin and I had created together. I convinced myself—and tried to convince my mother—that I could raise this baby. I didn't want to end another pregnancy. I looked at my mother, and she just stared into space. The doctor let me keep a copy of the ultrasound and went ahead with the procedure. Against my will, I underwent my third abortion in three years.

"After the abortion Kevin and I stayed away from each other for a couple of weeks. My girlfriends convinced me to go to the prom with them. Kevin went so far as to take another girl. That night when we saw each other, the sparks flew again. He took his date home and invited me to his hotel room that evening for a few hours.

"Kevin tried to explain his behavior. He told me that he lied to his parents about the baby not belonging to him because he was still angry with me. Kevin felt that I didn't do enough to prevent his juvenile trespassing charges. He told me that he had started seeing another girl to make sure he didn't get into any trouble for getting me pregnant again. He told me he was sorry and that he loved me. Kevin's excuses were believable to me and we rekindled our relationship."

Whitney looked at Deborah and Karen and said, "I wish I had used better judgment in making my decisions.

There were a thousand warning signs that Kevin was trouble, but love can be blinding—especially when you're young and naïve. My high school English teacher used to always say that 'good judgment comes from experience, and experience comes from bad judgment.' I now understand what she meant."

Whitney stood up and began straightening up the chairs in the classroom. She said goodnight to the two women, turned out the lights and headed home for the evening. She thought about the eight women who had attended the L.I.P.S. group tonight; at least one would end up back in the same abusive relationship she had already escaped from, and the whole cycle would begin again.

Staggering statistics darted through her head as she walked to her car. No matter how much she lectured and trained, it seemed like it wasn't enough. Whitney knew that somewhere in the country abusers were still victimizing other women. Every year, more than four

million women suffered abuse in the United States, resulting in three deaths per day. In 30 percent of those cases, the abuse was ongoing. There must be something more she could do, Whitney thought to herself. 'How many more women had to suffer; how many more women had to die?'

Chapter 4: "Warning Signs"

In retrospect, there was no excuse for me risking my life and staying in such a violent and unhealthy relationship with Kevin. But I still loved him. All the warning signs were there, but I chose to ignore them. I do believe there's a point of no return, where you're in too deep to get out on your own. It takes an act of God— or a life or death situation—to make you realize how desperate the situation has become.

My senior year of high school ushered in the opportunity for a fresh start. Kevin had been accepted to college in Virginia and was planning to leave at the end of the summer and start his freshman year. I was ready to have a normal life like all of my other teenage friends.

As was typical of our routine, Kevin and I got back together the night of our prom, and we were together all of the summer. Our parents had just given up on trying to keep us apart. I guess they were hoping this would be our last summer together since Kevin was going off to college.

As usual, our summers were great. It was as if we were the only two people who existed in the world. But as the summer came to an end, the old cycle started again. He would abuse me, force me to have sex, and control my every move.

Secretly, I hoped and prayed for the day that he would go away to college and find someone new— leaving me behind for good.

The week before Kevin left for school, he laid down the ground rules for our relationship. I could not have any male friends. I was not to socialize with any boys during the school day. I was to attend class, eat lunch and go home. I wasn't allowed to participate in any extracurricular activities, and hanging out with my friends was totally out of the question.

I was offered a spot on the cheerleading squad without even having to try out and he said "no." Kevin went so far as to pick out the clothes that were acceptable for me to wear.

Even after he left, he called every night to interrogate me: 'What did you do in class today? What did you wear to school? Who did you talk to? What time did you get home? Why did it take you so long to get home?' I had to repeat the same answers over and over until he was satisfied I was telling the truth. I was a prisoner in my own home, although he was hundreds of miles away. I spent my entire senior year in high school fighting with Kevin and missing out on some of the most fun and memorable events of my life.

I prayed that our relationship would get better, but it only got worse. I hoped that Kevin would relax and realize how much I truly loved him, but he didn't. His jealousy continued to grow, which only escalated the abuse when he came home on the weekends.

Since Kevin was away at college, he could no longer watch me and monitor my every move, so he found new ways to control me. I was working a part-time job to make some extra money, but most of that went to Kevin.

Although I was the one working and Kevin wasn't, he began controlling my paycheck. He would threaten me and force me to purchase all of his food and snacks to take back to school. Soon, most of the money I made was going to support him while he was away at college even though his parents were still funding his entire college education. The financial abuse became one more way for him to control me.

Initially, I thought college would put some distance between Kevin and me, but I was wrong. Every Friday, Kevin would come home with all his belongings, including the television. He would have brought the refrigerator too, but it wouldn't fit in the car. He didn't trust his roommates on campus, so every weekend he packed and unpacked—and returned home to terrorize me all over again.

One day Kevin picked me up and we were headed back to his house. I happened to glance at the car that was beside us at the light. By chance there happened to be a male driver in the car. Kevin immediately started accusing me of not only knowing this person but also of sleeping with him. I started to laugh because his accusations were outrageous to me. Kevin didn't see the humor. He took his fist and swung it right into my face. That resulted in my first black eye.

That evening after convincing him that what he was thinking was not true, he finally settled down and gave me an ice pack for my eye. Before it was all over, my eye had turned every color of the rainbow. I hid it for two weeks. But before my eye completely healed, one of my cousins saw me without make-up and told my mom the truth. She demanded an explanation.

I lied and told her that Kevin and I left a fast-food restaurant and he was driving too fast. As I leaned toward the dashboard to get the food out of the bag, Kevin slammed on brakes to avoid hitting another vehicle. I explained that my face smashed into the dashboard and I got a black eye—simple as that. My mom knew I was lying.

But no matter how bad things got, Kevin and I still loved each other and tried to make our relationship work. The routine continued. And each argument ended with Kevin apologizing profusely, begging me to take him back, and him telling me how much he loved me.

It was so predictable.

At home, things were still very tense between my parents. My mother began to spend more time away from home—in the company of other male friends. My stepfather seemed to be in his own world too. They spent so much time arguing, nobody noticed how badly I was hurting. My parents separated during my senior year. My mom moved out, and I made the choice to stay behind and live with my stepfather.

My stepfather had made me an offer I couldn't refuse. He said if I stayed with him and cooked and cleaned around the house, that he would allow Kevin to stay with me when he came home for the weekends. It was a no-brainer, and I readily accepted the offer. Since I had this newfound freedom, I figured Kevin wouldn't abuse me anymore. I was wrong. Since it was just my stepfather and me in the house all week, Kevin accused me of sleeping with him too—and then he punished me for it.

In situations this bad, things rarely get better without some type of intervention. One Friday evening when he had come home from school, Kevin was conducting his usual barrage of questioning. Except this particular time, he absolutely didn't believe a word I was saying. He was convinced my stepfather and I had been sleeping together all week.

The next thing I knew, he kicked me in the chest so hard that I flipped backwards across the bed and hit the floor. I was so outraged with him that I picked up a picture frame and threw it at him, and in the process I cut my finger so deeply I ended up having to get stitches. When my stepfather got home, he took me to the hospital. I knew he was suspicious that Kevin was still abusing me, but he never asked and I never told.

The abuse continued to escalate. The more I did to convince Kevin that I was faithful to him and loved him, the more suspicious and insecure he became. He began cutting me with dull knives to "teach me a lesson."

I remember one time when we had gone out and gotten into another argument. Kevin took me down a back road and made me get out of the car. There was a pile of empty beer bottles that he picked up and started throwing at me to punish me.

The harsh reality of the situation became apparent when he showed up at my part-time job unexpectedly, punched me in the face, fractured my nose and walked out as if he didn't do anything. I immediately fell to the floor. My supervisor ordered me to go to the hospital but I wouldn't. My girlfriend and her mother wanted me to press charges but I wouldn't.

They contacted my stepfather and let him know what had happened. I remember him coming in my room and sitting in my chair and saying, "If you don't leave this guy, he's going to kill you." And this time I believed him.

I broke off my relationship with Kevin. I had decided the abuse was more than I could handle. Of course he didn't make it easy on me, but I just ignored him and his phone calls and tried to move on with my life.

God has a funny way of getting your attention. Sometimes He speaks in a still, small voice, and other times, He speaks with lights, sirens and a megaphone. Unfortunately, I heard the warning two years earlier but ignored it. Finally I was getting the message.

One of my mother's friends Linda had been in an abusive relationship and told me that she'd be willing to listen if I ever wanted to talk. Everything I was going through, Linda had already experienced.

I really liked Linda. She was like that favorite cool aunt every kid wanted to stay with during the holidays or summer vacation. Linda was smart and funny and always had a smile on her face. Linda had two children, and her boyfriend Brian had four, from their previous marriages. How Linda ended up with someone like Brian, I'll never know.

I can recall my mom saying to me that Linda's aunt had passed away and the funeral was on Saturday. Linda and my mom had made plans to get together after the funeral. My mother told me that Linda had also left Brian. I guess she was fed up with the abuse and finally decided to leave.

Brian wasn't taking it well and didn't even pick up his paycheck that Friday. That was the first warning sign.

That Saturday morning Linda called the house. She wanted me to tell my mom to call her when she got home. They were still planning to get together later after her aunt's funeral. They never got the chance.

For the most part, the funeral service was uneventful. As they were lowering Linda's aunt into the ground, Brian walked up to Linda and said, "If I can't have you, no one will," and shot her close range in the chest. Brian then ran into the woods and shot himself in the head. Linda died at the gravesite.

Brian had four children, and Linda had two. Now both of them were dead, and six kids were left without their mother and father. I learned a valuable lesson that day about violence… it impacts everybody who's involved, and it has the ability to ruin several lives at once.

The reality of abuse kicked in when I saw Linda lying in that casket. I couldn't believe she was dead. I was expecting to see that big beautiful smile on her face but instead I saw a frown. My mom explained that when Linda saw Brian with that gun, she was so frightened that her last expression was a frown. The undertaker wasn't able to loosen the muscles on her face to make her smile again.

After Linda's funeral, I thought about her a lot. Her life had ended prematurely, and my life was on the exact same path. In the weeks before her death, Linda practically begged me to break up with Kevin, because she knew and understood what I was going through.

I knew that my situation was dire, but it never registered in my mind that Kevin might actually try to kill me. He loved me. 'How could you kill someone you really love,' I pondered in my mind.

On the other hand, a new sense of fear began to evolve in my mind. Some of the things that Brian had said to Linda, Kevin had also said to me. When she tried to leave, she ended up dead. Could the same thing really happen to me? I knew that breaking up with him would only make matters worse, but I was willing to take a chance. Linda's death was a wake-up call, but how long would I listen?

By spring, I could see the light of graduation at the end of the tunnel. I had applied and been accepted to community college and saw this as my chance to get away from Kevin and start a new life. This relationship had stolen my youth and my high school years, but I didn't want to lose out on the college years too.

Each year at high school, the tradition of "senior skip day" continued. That was the one time students could skip class without fear of punishment or retribution. My girlfriends and I went to the lake for a day of fun. Since the college students had already gotten out for the summer, that meant Kevin was free to crash the event—and he did. Several of the guys in my class took it upon themselves to keep him away from me, because of course, everybody knew about "the fighting couple."

It was well known that Kevin and I were officially broken up. The guys at the lake from my school had put enough of a scare in him to keep him away from me. I was confident that this phase of my life was finally ending, and a brand new chapter was beginning.

At the end of my senior year, I got my first taste of true independence. My mom and stepdad had reconciled and rekindled their relationship and were making plans to move to Georgia—without me. The relationship between my grandmother and me had deteriorated because of the choice I made to stay with my stepfather instead of my mother when they first split up. I guess that was the equivalent of treason as far as family was concerned.

And as for my real father, I hadn't heard from him or spoken to him in years. Now, I was alone, but not for long.

Kevin came back into my life on my graduation day. He told me that all the time we had spent away from each other made him see the error of his ways and he vowed never to abuse me again.

He told me how much he loved me and how he couldn't live without me. We were adults now, I reasoned, and surely we could make our relationship work. I believed he had taken my leaving him seriously and that he wouldn't harm me again. Now that we were no longer subject to our parents' rules or their attempts to break us up, we could start a new life together.

Deep down I knew that going back to Kevin would be the biggest mistake of my life. But I fell for his game, and we got back together.

Love makes you do crazy things. The summer of 1992 seemed like the hottest year on record. I had graduated from high school on the same Saturday that my parents moved to Georgia. That evening Kevin and I spent the night in a hotel making plans for our future. I was planning to go to college in the fall and Kevin was returning only if he got a new car to go along with him.

That Sunday I was scheduled to go to work but Kevin convinced me not to go and to spend the day with him. As we were pulling away from my job, unbeknownst to me, my boss saw me leave. Needless to say, I got fired. I guess I should have seen it coming. There were many instances where I had to call in sick— or hurt—because of my past injuries from Kevin. My supervisor finally had enough. And when I called in to inform her that I wouldn't be at work that day, she informed me that I no longer had a job.

I graduated on Saturday, got fired on Sunday, and was homeless on Monday. By this time, my parents had moved, my grandmother had disowned me, and Kevin was all I had left.

When Kevin's parents refused to buy him a new car, he rebelled and refused to go back to school. And since he refused to go to school, they stopped paying his way. The two of us were on our own.

Kevin and I lived together in his car for the entire summer.

He wasn't working, and neither was I. He didn't have any money, and neither did I.

Every morning after Kevin's parents left for work, we broke into their house to take showers and raid the refrigerator. During the day, we parked behind an abandoned warehouse to conserve gas and stay cool. We got dinner by begging for food from our friends who worked at the local fast-food restaurants. And Kevin made me beg for money from our family and friends each week. At night, we slept in the hospital parking lot.

Everything I owned was in the trunk of the car. I didn't think things could get much worse… but of course, they did. The heat only intensified the friction between us. He was now able to dictate my life again, and I didn't have enough confidence and independence to defy his orders. In his mind, everything was 'the world according to Kevin.'

And when I violated his world order, there was a hefty price to pay. I felt like a prisoner. Kevin blamed everything on me, and I had the bruises to prove it.

One morning, we went over to his parents' house, but his mother hadn't left yet. She saw us outside and flagged down the car. Enough was enough. They wanted Kevin to come back home and go to school. I still had nowhere to go. His parents agreed that I could stay with them for one week while I found somewhere else to live. After that week was up, Kevin continued to sneak me in through his bedroom window and made me sleep on the floor in his tiny bedroom closet. One night I just couldn't take it anymore and fell asleep on the bed. When his parents realized I was still staying in their house, they kicked me out.

I decided to take matters into my own hands. I called my cousin in Richmond, VA, and asked her to come get me. I didn't talk it over with Kevin. I just knew it was time to go. I missed the deadline to register for school, so instead I moved to Virginia.

At his parents' urging, Kevin got a job working at a health club. Since they weren't getting him a new car, and he wasn't going back to school, he had to do something. He started making a pretty decent sales commission and talked me into moving back home so we could start a life together.

The same vicious cycle began all over again. Kevin sent me a bus ticket, and I came home on a Saturday. He got fired the following Monday, and I was right back where I started. I didn't have anything, and I didn't have anywhere to go.

We went back to the lake in my old hometown and had a very long conversation. We decided to get away and make a fresh start. Instead of going to college and pursuing our dreams, we were learning how to survive.

Kevin and I packed up all our belongings and drove to a small town called Bridgewater about an hour away.

I didn't know many people there, but I remembered that my mom had lived there when she separated from my stepdad, so I followed in her footsteps and contacted her former landlord.

There was a boutique at the Bridgewater Mall. I got an interview and was offered a job right on the spot. I called another cousin in New York and asked her to send me money to get my first apartment. Kevin got a part-time job at a nearby store in the mall. Finally, things were coming together, and Kevin and I moved into our first place together.

Our new home was a dingy little studio apartment that was about 600 square feet. It wasn't much, but it was ours; actually, it was mine, because everything was in my name. Everybody around us was poor, and we were too.

We didn't have any furniture at all. Old flowered bed sheets from my childhood twin bed hung on the wall as curtains. We didn't have a bed, so we slept on an old mattress on the living room floor and watched three channels on Kevin's 13-inch color television set.

Of course, Kevin wasn't satisfied, and felt as if this "rat hole" was beneath him. He constantly whined and complained. He didn't like the apartment. He didn't like our neighbors. He didn't like the landlord. He didn't like my job. He didn't like my co-workers.

The more frustrated he became, the more violent his behavior became. To relieve his frustration, he would hit me and then force me to have sex. Now that we were living together, saying "no" to him was pointless.

Neither of us was ready to have a baby, but we didn't have enough money to afford birth control. When I found out that I was pregnant again, I got a second job. After the physical and mental strain of having three abortions, ending this pregnancy was not an option. Every day I worked from 8:00 to 2:00 in the afternoon as a clerk at the local drugstore, and then went to the boutique from 3:00 to 9:00 in the evening.

Kevin lost his job at the electronics store in the mall, so I became the sole provider for our household. He, on the other hand, sat around the house all day watching television and coming up with things to argue about. He refused to go back to school, and he refused to work. He literally just sat around and sulked.

We didn't have enough money to purchase anything extra. The rent and grocery bills took almost everything we had. I couldn't afford maternity clothes, so I wore Kevin's sweatshirts and old school clothes to work. I applied for public assistance to get proper prenatal treatment during my pregnancy. Kevin was furious that I "stooped so low" as to ask for outside help. But since he wasn't working or earning any money, there wasn't much for him to say.

By working at the mall, I began to meet a lot of people and make a lot of new friends. This enraged Kevin. For whatever reason, he continued to think that I was cheating on him. His insecurities just continued to grow and wreak havoc on our already strained relationship. I thought having a child together would make Kevin grow up, act more mature and treat me better. But instead, it had the opposite effect. Somehow he knew that by having his baby, I would never leave him. He knew how I felt about wanting to keep my family together, so that gave him free reign to act however he wanted and take all of his frustrations out on me.

Kevin still slapped me and pushed me around until my pregnancy began to show. The blatant physical abuse began to subside as the pregnancy progressed, but the mental, verbal and emotional abuse increased. Since he didn't want to risk hurting the baby, Kevin had to find other ways to control me by keeping me in a state of constant fear and vulnerability.

He started to become even more controlling and possessive. He became very clingy; he didn't want me to be out of his sight or even talk to another man—

including my physician. He came with me to every doctor's appointment I had, and even stayed in the room during my entire OB/GYN visits.

One day my doctor wanted to question me without Kevin in the room, but Kevin wasn't going for it. He stated that if the doctor had anything to ask me, he could ask me in front of Kevin. The doctor asked if everything was OK because rarely had he seen a young father come to every prenatal visit. It was peculiar, to say the least.

I was a little offended by the question, but Kevin told him off quite well. Although the physician was right about something being wrong, I didn't say a word. At the time, I didn't see it as a problem. I was just glad Kevin was happy about the baby, and relieved that he wasn't hitting, slapping or beating me every day.

As any mother knows, being pregnant in the summertime is miserable under the best circumstances. Being pregnant, broke, overworked, tired and abused in the summertime is decidedly unbearable. The nature of our relationship was that of gasoline and a lighted match waiting to connect.

Near the end of my pregnancy, it was difficult for me to drive to work, so occasionally Kevin would drop me off and pick me up in the evenings. One day, when he put the car in reverse, it didn't move. The engine continued to rev, but the car didn't budge. Kevin looked under the hood and informed me that the reverse gear had blown out. We didn't have the money to get it fixed, so Kevin just pushed the car backward into the street, until I could shift into drive and move forward.

Just when he got the car moving again, I informed him that I had to use the bathroom—a symptom common for expectant moms. He was infuriated. He got out of the car and pushed it backwards so that he could turn back into the driveway. He ordered me to hurry up while he waited outside. I finished and waddled back to the driver's side and got in. Kevin pushed the car back into the street so we could get moving again. I wanted to laugh, but I knew that would start a fight.

Kevin got back in the driver's seat and started to adjust the rearview mirror. He used a little too much force and the mirror broke off and fell on the floor. We just sat there quietly for a moment. Kevin was furious. He started cursing. Without a moment's hesitation, he threw the broken rearview mirror towards the back of the car and shattered the back windshield. I screamed and ducked to keep from getting hit by shards of flying glass. For a while, we rode around with broken glass in the back seat. We bought some duct tape and clear plastic to cover up the open window.

Kevin hated the car by this point, but it was the only transportation we had. He was still furious that his parents had refused to buy him a new one. And each week, something different went wrong with the car. By the end of June, the car had no reverse, no air conditioning, no rearview mirror, no back windshield and no headlights. We were a traffic accident waiting to happen.

The police stopped us at least 10 times about the poor condition of the car we were driving. We got warning tickets, citations and threats to have the car towed if we didn't get it fixed. On a quick drive to the grocery store, I got pulled over again. The officer looked familiar because he had pulled us over several weeks ago. He approached me on the driver's side.

"Good afternoon, ma'am. Do you know why I pulled you over?"

"Yes sir. Because of the broken windshield."

"Yes ma'am. But I also stopped you a few weeks ago and told you to get this car fixed. Why haven't you gotten it fixed yet?"

"Sir, I don't have the money."

"Did you get those headlights fixed yet?"

"No sir."

"Well, I hate to do this to you, but I'm going to have to have the car towed. Do you understand?"

I didn't say anything.

"Ma'am, do you understand?"

Silence.

"Ma'am, are you OK?"

I started breathing in short, shallow breaths and rubbing my stomach. "Aaah," I screamed. "Oh my God, I felt a contraction. I think I'm going into labor!"

"OK, ma'am, just calm down. Do you need me to call an ambulance?"

"No, I just need to get home and lay down. I can call my doctor from there. I live just a couple of miles from here, but I really need to get going officer."

"All right, ma'am, I'm going to let you go, but the next time I catch you out here in this vehicle without the necessary repairs, I'm going to have you towed. Do you understand?"

"Yes sir. Thank you, sir. Have a good day."

I sped off and headed toward the grocery store, relieved that I didn't get another traffic ticket.

I had kept my pregnancy a secret once again until I was about five months pregnant. We had decided to keep this baby and start a family. One Sunday afternoon Kevin's parents showed up at the house unexpectedly, so of course, I couldn't hide it any longer. They were happy for us and wanted to make sure everything was coming along fine with the baby. After their visit I decided to let the rest of the family know too. I even contacted my biological father. The baby was due in the month of July so my cousin even planned a baby shower for the 4th of July celebration.

A couple of weeks before the baby was due we decided to move to a much nicer apartment. Kevin's parents had given us their old bedroom, living room and kitchen set. My grandmother even gave us some real curtains to put up. It still wasn't what Kevin was used to, but he was a little happier.

I worked up until the very day I went into labor. After 24 long and intense hours of labor, our first child— a beautiful and healthy baby girl named Brianna—was born on July 3rd. The birth of my first child was bittersweet due to the fact that on that same day, my great grandmother was being buried. She had died at the age of 103. Life has such strange coincidences; the passing of one life ushered in the beginning of another.

I was able to come home the next day and the baby shower went on as planned. We received so many nice new things for the baby. We had everything we needed, so I didn't have to buy a thing.

Kevin's parents realized that having a child together would forever create a bond between their son and me. And now that we were living together and had a child as part of the equation, they finally decided to reach out to us. Concerned for the safety of their first grandchild, his parents topped the baby shower off by giving us a used car. It was a nice car—nothing too fancy—but the headlights and all the gears worked, and it had air conditioning and a back windshield.

Having a new car was the first of many steps in the right direction for us. We had a new apartment, and I got a new job that paid more and provided health benefits. We saved money on daycare by letting Kevin stay home and take care of our daughter. Despite our progress, it still wasn't enough for Kevin.

With a new baby in the house, I realized that Kevin was a much better father to our child than he was as a boyfriend to me. He loved our daughter and cared for her every need. In spite of the difficulties in our relationship, being a father was the one thing he was excited about.

More than anything, I think Kevin resented the fact that he hadn't finished school and become a lawyer or a professional basketball player. I knew he blamed me. Minimum wage positions were an insult to him, and he honestly felt that they were beneath him. So rather than "settle" for less than what he wanted, Kevin decided to stay at home and do nothing at all.

My work ethic was very different from Kevin's. Growing up, I saw how materialism could destroy a family, and I made a decision early on to work for what I wanted. I didn't feel like I was better than anybody else, and I was willing to do whatever it took to provide for my family. On the other hand, Kevin grew up with a sense of entitlement—and felt as if the world somehow owed him something.

Things began to fall in place, so we took another step in the "right direction." Like most little girls, I had dreamed about meeting my Prince Charming and how he would sweep me off my feet and get down on one knee to propose to me. I envisioned a beautiful church wedding where I wore a radiant white wedding gown and a stunning veil. Our family and friends would come to witness me and my fiancé exchange our wedding vows and commit the rest of our lives to each other.

Then I woke up.

A PrintHouse Books; Non-Fiction Title

With the new baby and a new car we decided to mend some family relationships and go visit my biological father in New York. My family and I were all sitting around talking, and one of my aunts suggested that Kevin and I get married.

"Whitney, you and Kevin have a child together now. Why don't you do the right thing and make it official?"

Kevin and I just looked at each other. He shrugged his shoulders and turned back to watch the football game on television. When I told my biological father that we were getting married, he took Kevin aside in the room and spoke with him for a while.

I never knew what their conversation was about. I can remember my father asking me whether I was sure about my decision. He let me know that just because I had a child with Kevin didn't mean that I had to marry him. I confirmed that my decision was final and asked him to walk me down the aisle.

On the drive back home Kevin and I discussed wedding plans. With the date being set for that following

July, we had less than a year to prepare. Of course, I did all of the work. Kevin never did propose to me.

Considering everything we had been through, who would have thought I would marry Kevin? I knew that I loved him, but honestly, that wasn't enough. From the time I was a little girl and realized how much it hurt me not having both of my parents in my life, I was determined that if I ever had children, I would make my relationship work. I absolutely did not want my children growing up without one of their parents.

So, I swallowed my pride and convinced myself that everything was OK. The whole time I was planning for the wedding, Kevin and I didn't fight. It was as if I had finally found the man I had fallen in love with in high school. I believed he would be a good father and husband. I got married as much for my little girl as I did for myself.

We had an outdoor wedding in my grandmother's yard. Our wedding was the day before Brianna's first birthday. Everyone seemed happy for us. Although they knew how difficult the relationship had been on our families in the past, Kevin's parents were supportive and helped pay for the wedding. My biological father walked me down the aisle and gave us $1,500 to help us start a new life together. To this day, I still don't know why I asked him to walk me down the aisle instead of my stepfather who had been there for me when I needed him. But I know my stepdad was upset because he didn't attend the wedding.

My mom didn't contribute anything other than looking worried, and my grandmother didn't say anything at all. Kevin seemed preoccupied and uninterested in the wedding. It didn't seem like he really cared about getting married one way or the other. As long as we were together, that was good enough for him.

I took my wedding vows seriously. And when I said the words, "for better or worse," I really meant them. I wanted my marriage to work, and I was willing to do whatever was necessary to keep my family together. Our "marital bliss" was short-lived.

Kevin had made reservations at a hotel a few hours away for our honeymoon. In order to save money, we decided to keep things simple. For the first hour, the conversation was fairly light and entertaining. I talked about the ceremony, and he talked about how much money people had given us for our wedding. Then the tone of the conversation changed after it appeared that we had gotten lost.

"Where is this damn hotel," Kevin asked angrily.

"I don't know. You didn't tell me where we were going, so I can't help you," I replied. "Don't get smart with me," he said. "Well, why don't you just stop and ask somebody since we're lost," I said.

Before the words were completely out of my mouth, I felt the palm of Kevin's hand go across the side of my face. At first I felt a stinging sensation on my jaw, and then the reality of what happened set in. My new husband had just hit me on our wedding night. I thought to myself, "What in the hell have I done?" We rode around lost for another hour before we finally found the hotel.

We didn't really talk or spend any quality time together the rest of the night. Kevin watched the game on television, and I just went to bed wondering how I could have married this man.

After our honeymoon, things went back to normal, and the beatings continued. Kevin became increasingly jealous of me because I had gotten a new job, enrolled in community college and was making strides to get ahead. By now, I had learned how to play the game. I hid my emotions, and I hid the scars. I didn't tell anyone what was going on. I was determined that my life was going to be successful one way or the other.

On the other hand, Kevin's temper and volatile personality made him a difficult employee, and he rarely kept a job for more than four or five months. He usually got fired for his bad attitude and for insubordination. He was determined to make things difficult one way or another.

Kevin became more self-absorbed and was easily irritated by the slightest things. He started experiencing weird physical symptoms and spent a lot of time in the doctor's office. He was eventually diagnosed with stomach ulcers—brought on by stress—and then misdiagnosed with a sexually transmitted disease.

No matter what I said, it didn't seem to deter Kevin from thinking that in between work, school, and putting up with his foolishness on a daily basis, I somehow found the time and energy to have an affair.

"Whitney, get over here now," he screamed when he showed up at my job unexpectedly.

"Kevin, what are you doing here," I asked.

My co-workers had curious and concerned looks on their faces. Only my supervisor knew that I was in an abusive situation. The others just thought this type of behavior was inappropriate.

"The doctor says I have an STD, so I want to know who you've been sleeping with!"

"Can we talk about this at another time? This is my place of employment—are you trying to get me fired or something?" I was looking around anxiously to see if my supervisor was aware of what was going on. I knew somebody was going to tell him, and I wasn't sure if I'd still have a job the next day.

"No, we're going to talk about it now. I want an explanation!"

"What are you talking about? I'm not sleeping with anybody except you. I would never cheat on you.

I managed to lead him back outside the store so we wouldn't be the main attraction for the customers and employees. He stood about an inch from me, and I could feel him literally breathing down my neck.

In a sharp and whispered tone, he said slowly, "Don't play games with me! I'm going to ask you again. Who have you been sleeping with? Answer me! The doctor doesn't know me from anybody, and he has no reason to lie. He said that if I have an STD, then I probably got it from you, because I haven't been with anybody else." Kevin grabbed my arm and squeezed it tightly. I started slowly backing up toward the door so that my co-workers could still see me, and I felt my heart pounding against my chest. For a moment, I really believed that Kevin was going to kill me.

The store manager came out and asked if I was OK and whether or not there was a problem. Kevin said, "No sir, there's not a problem; but there's going to be one."

Kevin rolled his eyes at me and said, "Just wait until you get home." Then he turned and left.

All the color had drained from my face, and I was shaking all over. I was afraid to go home that night.

When Kevin picked me up from work, I was terrified. He didn't miss a beat and picked up right where we left off. Kevin was furious, even though I hadn't done anything wrong. Admittedly, I was curious about how he got an STD. It was bad enough that he was abusing me. The thought of him cheating on me too was downright insulting.

When we got home, I ran straight to our neighbors' apartment, pounding on their front door and begging them to let me in. I didn't know what was going to happen to me once I got inside with Kevin. Although they were at home, nobody came to the door. That made a very bad situation worse. Kevin was angry because I had made a scene and because I had tried to involve outsiders in our "family business." He didn't hit me that night—probably because he knew the neighbors were listening.

The next day, Kevin's physician called to apologize and to inform him that the office laboratory technicians had made a mistake. Instead of an STD, he actually had a urinary tract infection, and there was nothing to be concerned about. That phone call saved my life because Kevin felt he finally had his concrete evidence and surely would have beat me to death. Even after the physician called, Kevin never apologized to me.

As I approached the end of my first semester, I was on top of the world. Two weeks before final exams, I found out I was pregnant again, and nose-dived into a deep state of depression. I quit going to school, and received an "Incomplete" in every class I was taking— which only compounded my depression. I cried constantly and practically stopped eating. On the bright side, at least by being pregnant again I wouldn't have to deal with as much abuse.

Once again I worked up until the day I had the baby. I had just gotten home from work and immediately went into labor. Kevin wasn't there for the birth. He had dropped me off at the hospital and took Brianna to my grandmother's house and didn't make it back in time.

The birth of our second child—a handsome baby boy named Asa—gave me a false sense of security that everything would be OK. Kevin still seemed to enjoy fatherhood. And as long as he was focused on taking care of the kids, he was fine. Kevin's parents were happy to be grandparents again, but quickly expressed that we should not be having anymore children for a while.

I can remember visiting his parents and hearing them always getting on him about not working and not supporting his family. Kevin always left their house feeling like a failure. Once again, it was all my fault that he wasn't successful, so he would intimidate me by threatening to hit me or acting as if he was going to hit me.

For months, I would ride in the car with my hands and leg covering my face to prepare myself for his blows. Kevin thrived off of controlling me. Beating me became a sport to him. He came up with new ways to terrorize me and began hitting me on my back and upper body to hide the bruises. All the while our two children rode in the back seat.

With me working so much and not having time to cook (and Kevin not liking most of the meals I prepared anyway), we started eating fast food every night. And the more we ate out, the more Kevin capitalized on every opportunity to find something wrong with our food. Once, there was a fly in his drink, and we got money. There was a rubber band in our pizza crust; we got money. There was a bug floating in our tea; we got money. I thought to myself that if Kevin would apply that much effort and creativity to a job, we'd be all right.

My life was nothing like what I had planned. I was only 20 years old, and I was married to a con artist who abused me in one way or another every day. I had dropped out of school, and I was now a new mother of two children. I just kept telling myself things were going to get better.

I went back to work full time exactly one week after I gave birth. I was now the store manager, because my boss quit while I was on "maternity leave." Financially speaking, I couldn't afford to be at home since Kevin wasn't working. I wasn't sure how much worse things could get so I just focused on taking care of the kids and doing a good job at work. Working gave me a reason to get out of the house—and away from Kevin.

With me spending so much time at work, I got to know my customers by name and I will always remember one lady in particular. Her name was Maria and she was a teacher's assistant who just loved shopping at my store. Maria came in the store everyday after work with her daughter. I don't think her daughter was any older than 11 or 12. Maria didn't necessarily buy clothes everyday, she would come by just to look—or to chat.

One day I can remember her coming in the store and telling me that she and her new husband were expecting their first child together. She was so excited! And then out of the blue, I didn't see her anymore.

Months went by and one day Maria's daughter came in the store with someone else. Smiling, I said to her, "Girl, where is your mother?" "You better tell her to get in here to see me." I'll never forget her daughter's words to me: "Momma's dead." I didn't know what to say. The lady she was with was her stepmother, who went on to tell me that Maria's husband had killed her. Apparently he wasn't as happy about the baby as Maria was. In fact he didn't even believe that the baby was his, so he tied

Maria to the bed, sliced her throat, cut the baby out of her stomach, doused the bed in gasoline, and set Maria and their house on fire.

I was in shock for days. I just couldn't believe what had happened. I couldn't even sleep because Maria was constantly on my mind. I thought to myself that she and I had a lot more in common than I realized. This was yet another wake-up call that I would inevitably ignore. I didn't believe that Kevin would really try to kill me—did I?

A few months after the birth of our son, Kevin got a real job selling cars at a dealership 45 minutes away. We moved so he could be closer to work. For the first time, he was making the kind of money he had dreamed about and was able to provide the kind of lifestyle he always wanted.

Kevin got a signing bonus and a company car. We moved into an upscale luxury apartment community, we purchased a new car, and started giving our kids the best things that money could buy. I didn't think our children would be as rotten as Kevin and Kendall, but in actuality, mine were worse. Every Christmas they had more gifts than they could open.

They had more clothes and shoes than I did, and I worked everyday. Now Kevin was able to purchase clothes and shoes from the same company in California that his parents once did. He had fancy jewelry and almost everything he wanted. I never went shopping. In fact, I hated shopping. And even when we had the money, I never bought myself anything. Materialistic things never meant much to me.

As I look back, I realize that the most important things you can give your kids—money will never be able to buy.

But when Kevin had money, things seemed to improve. We spent time together as a family; we went to the park, we ate out at nice restaurants, and we did all the things that most families do. For a while, Kevin was OK. And when he was OK, I was OK.

My whole focus in life was to make sure that Kevin got whatever he wanted—whenever he wanted it. If his food wasn't prepared just the way he liked it, he would make me throw it out and cook something else for him. If he didn't like what was on television, I would change the channel for him. If he didn't like something I bought at the store, I would immediately take it back and replace it. As long as he was happy, we were all happy.

All I wanted was my sanity; that's all I really needed. But the moment he was unhappy, life became very unpleasant for everyone around him. Kevin was showing the same selfish and self-centered behavior that he had in high school. It had to be his way, or no way at all.

His attitude made everything more complicated than it needed to be. Nothing satisfied him. We hired and fired eight different babysitters in two months because Kevin found something about each one of them that he didn't like. After a while, it seemed as if he didn't like me anymore because I wasn't good enough either.

I watched our relationship transform before my eyes. There were a lot of changes. We were now married with two children. And for the first time ever, Kevin was working and I was at home with the kids. He now had all the control. I had quit my job at the department store to cater to Kevin's needs and to stay home with our children since we couldn't find a suitable babysitter or daycare center—according to him.

There's something about a woman's intuition that lets her know when things aren't right. And I knew something wasn't right. Kevin began spending a lot more time working late and away from home. I dared not question him about it because that would only start another fight. He also seemed a little too friendly with one of our female neighbors.

Giving birth to two babies and staying at home during the days had helped me add on an extra 40 pounds. When I looked in the mirror, I told myself I was fat. I could tell that Kevin was disgusted by the way I looked. He stopped paying attention to me and sometimes didn't even acknowledge my presence. At night, instead of coming to bed, he would fall asleep on the couch.

We didn't even sleep in the same bed any longer. He would spend hours playing games with the children, and hardly spoke to me at all. I always felt that he was involved with more than one woman, but I never confronted him about it.

Now that he had money and a measurable level of success, he didn't need me anymore.

One day the kids and I were at the grocery store around the corner from Kevin's job. As I was shutting the door, I quickly realized I was locking the keys in the car. When I went to open it my index finger got caught in the door. Blood was everywhere, and I thought I had almost sliced off my finger. I got back in the car and was able to make it to Kevin's job. My intention was for him to drive me to the hospital since I was in so much pain. Instead of sympathy I got ridiculed. Not only did Kevin make me wait for him to give his clients to someone else, he was angry for having to leave work and take me to the hospital.

Kevin was one of the top salesmen at the dealership, and he won a lot of bonuses and trips in exchange for his efforts. For him, it was all about the money. He even sold a car to his parents and made a profit from the sale. Kevin was now bragging to his parents that he made more money than they did and that he clearly wasn't a failure. In his world, second best was unacceptable.

His first year, he earned more money than he ever had. During a weekend sales campaign he won an all-expense-paid trip to attend the Olympics. On this trip we got a chance to mingle with the stars. We were even able to see the "Dream Team" play basketball.

This was the life that Kevin really wanted. The day before returning back home, he told me that he was tired of working at the dealership and that he now wanted to pursue his acting career. I supported Kevin 100 percent. But when I told him that the kids and I would stay behind so I could work and continue to support our family, he changed his mind. Once again, he blamed me for holding him back from his dream.

Although he was the top salesman, Kevin had also received two write-ups for insubordination and was put on probation for his negative attitude and inability to work as part of a team. Kevin didn't get along with his co-workers at the car dealership, and after a year (his longest job ever), he was fired from that job too.

Two days later, Kevin walked in the front door and announced that he had gotten another job selling cars with a manager friend from his former job.

That lasted about three weeks—long enough to get the signing bonus and some additional free sales training. This became a cycle that Kevin repeated three or four times. He would get hired at a dealership, work long enough to qualify for the signing bonus, and then quit.

We were clearly living above our means, but Kevin was determined that anything less than the best was unacceptable, whether we could afford it or not. Instead of moving to a less expensive apartment and reducing our budget, Kevin bought another car. It was his dream car, and it cost us $450 per month.

He lied on the application about his income and employment and got approved for the car loan. Kevin wrote a down-payment check for $1,000. We both knew that the money was not in the bank. I would have to figure out how to pay both car notes.

Life is full of irony. The night we bought the car, Kevin wanted to take it out for a spin. We had barely made it out of the dealership parking lot, when out of nowhere, a late-night driver slammed into the rear-end of the vehicle. The other driver had fallen asleep at the wheel and lost control of the car. Thankfully, no one was hurt. But the car was wrecked. When Kevin jumped out of the car, he was so enraged, I really believed that he was going to kill the other driver.

Kevin was breathing so hard, I thought he might hyperventilate.

"Look what you did to my car, you idiot! This car is brand new. I can't believe you hit my brand new car with that piece of junk you're driving. Look what you did! What in the hell were you thinking?"

The other driver was panicking because Kevin was so out of control. "I'm sorry. I'm really sorry. I just got off of work, and I worked a double shift. I fell asleep at the wheel, and I lost control of the car. I'm sorry, sir. I just couldn't stop in time. I'm so sorry."

Kevin screamed, "You're sorry? You're sorry? You're gonna be sorry, all right. You wait until I get my hands on you." He started to approach the man.

I jumped out of the car and tried to intervene, "Kevin, it was an accident. It's just a car; we can get it fixed. Everybody's OK. Please just calm down."

"Whitney, get back in the car and stay out of this. I'll handle this myself," he said.

The other driver got back in his car and locked the doors to wait for the police.

Kevin stood outside the man's car door cursing at him until the police arrived. I was beyond embarrassed for Kevin, for the other driver, and for our family. I just sat in the car and held my head down.

When the police arrived, Kevin was still ranting and raving about his precious car being destroyed. Then, he started complaining about his neck hurting. I could almost see the wheels turning in his head trying to figure out how to make money out of the situation.

The police checked his neck for injuries and took statements from both Kevin and the other driver. The man explained to them that he had fallen asleep, so there wasn't much they could do but give him a citation. That wasn't good enough for Kevin, and he was furious for days.

Although the other driver's insurance covered the expenses for repairs and medical bills, Kevin still wasn't satisfied. We both went to the doctor for minor back problems, but we didn't get the car fixed. Instead we used the money to pay bills and buy groceries. Our situation was declining quickly, and that meant the violence would increase.

I immediately got a job in another clothing store. Kevin constantly reminded me that my salary was nothing compared to what he had been earning. There was no way that I could maintain our living expenses by myself. Kevin drifted in and out of depression because he wasn't making big money any longer and because his beloved car had been hit. He sat at home running up the phone bill calling California about potential acting gigs that never materialized.

During this time, the O.J. Simpson trial was going on and Kevin spent all day watching that and all night watching the NBA playoff games and the "Real World" reality television show. He started sulking again and whining that he could have been a famous lawyer, professional basketball player or actor.

Our reality was that the kids needed diapers and food, and we had to keep a roof over our heads. Kevin had alienated his parents, and wouldn't dare call to inform them that he had lost his job.

On the other hand, things went well for me at work, and I got promoted to assistant store manager in a matter of weeks. They gave me a small raise and increased my responsibilities. I started supervising two other part-time employees and became friends with one of my co¬workers, Meredith. She had a son my daughter's age and a fiancé too, so we had a lot in common. They even came over to our apartment during happier times.

Despite my best efforts, the bills kept coming and I wasn't able to cover them. The landlord terminated our lease and filed a notice of eviction. My car financing company sent out a notice to repossess; and repossession of Kevin's car wasn't too far behind. He was still unemployed while I was worked overtime to keep our family afloat. Pleasant conversations in our house were few and far between.

"Kevin, why don't we just sell the cars and get a less expensive one," I asked. "You know for a fact that we can't afford this stuff anymore. Let's just sell the cars and

move. You're not bringing any money into this house, so we need to cut down our expenses."

The mere suggestion of having to return something that he loved was met with sheer indignation. He said, "I don't care what you think, I'm not selling my car. I love that car, and I'm not letting it go. The money will be there by the time the check clears."

It wasn't.

"I'm not writing a check for money we don't have," I shouted.

He raised his voice and practically demanded that I drop the whole issue. "Listen, Whitney, I'm not going to say this again. I am not selling my car, and I'm not moving back to some dump like where we were before. I'm not gonna let my kids live just anywhere. They deserve the best, and that's what I'm going to give them. Do you understand?"

I responded, "Kevin, that doesn't make any sense. We can't afford to stay here, and you know my check isn't big enough to cover all these bills. I can barely afford to buy food. We've got to do something. Would you just listen to me for once?" My voice was trembling from the fear and anger I felt for him. He was being absolutely unreasonable.

Instinctively, I knew what was going to happen next. When I saw both of his hands coming toward me, I ducked to miss the blow. Then I felt the force of all his weight against my shoulders when he shoved me into the wall. My back hit the wall first, and then my head. I slid down the wall until I hit the floor. I raised my arms to protect my head and face and begged him to stop. I silently prayed that my daughter didn't come out of her room and see me cowering in a corner—afraid of her father.

Just when it seemed like things couldn't get much worse, I found out that I was pregnant again. Kevin begged and pleaded, coerced and threatened me into an abortion. He absolutely did not want any more children, and his fist made a persuasive argument.

I knew financially we couldn't afford another child, but mentally and physically, I couldn't afford to have another abortion. Ultimately, he won. The trip to the doctor's office was becoming familiar. The guilt that I felt as a mother making that decision was enormous.

I never told Kevin how I really felt because I knew it wouldn't matter. He was adamant about ending the pregnancy, and I knew it was a losing battle.

During this summer my cousins had all come down to visit and wanted to get together for a cookout at the lake. Kevin didn't want to go, so the kids and I went without him. When I got home, Kevin was furious and he immediately started hitting me and berating me for hanging out with my cousins all day. He locked me in the room and didn't let me out until he decided I had learned my lesson.

The hours that I spent alone "taking my punishment" gave me time to think and to convince myself I needed to leave this relationship. When Kevin finally let me out, I called 911 to get help. He snatched the receiver from me and quickly hung up the phone. I knew that the 911 operator would call right back to make sure everything was OK, but Kevin told the operator that our daughter had been playing with the phone and dialed them by accident. They believed him, so the police didn't come.

Shortly thereafter, I made my first official attempt to leave the relationship. A couple of days later I called the local battered women's shelter only to be informed that they were full. Even though they weren't able to give my children and me a safe place to stay, they referred me to a local church.

When I contacted the church, they told me that we would have to sleep on church pews and that they would watch the children for me while I worked during the day. I didn't want my children to have to live that way. I didn't want them to leave their cozy beds to sleep on church pews. I knew that I had to leave Kevin, but I wanted to make sure the kids would have a comfortable life. So I endured almost another year of Kevin's abuse until I was able to leave and never return. The good times were long gone.

The tougher things got, the more abusive Kevin became. We started repeating our old cycle again. We'd argue. He'd hit me. Then he'd force me to have sex. Argue. Abuse. Sex. 'No' never meant 'no'. We weren't using any kind of protection or birth control, so three months later, I was pregnant again with my youngest son. This time, I put my foot down and told Kevin that we were having the baby. We did.

In the meantime, our rent and other bills fell even further behind.

I argued for weeks about the first worthless check Kevin wrote to the car dealership. After that one, the second check became easier to write, even though we didn't have the money. The check was written to our landlord in the amount of $1,000 to cover the past-due rent. It bounced, just like the down-payment check for Kevin's car.

The situation was critical, and Kevin told me that I had better do something to fix it. He had an idea, and I was too afraid of him not to go along with it.

Every night we made cash deposits at the store where I worked. I was familiar with the schedule and knew when the most money came in. Kevin assured me that he was not going to give up his car, so I had to do something to keep the peace. We owed a little more than $900—including the late fees. Kevin told me to steal the Saturday night deposit from the store where I worked and use the money to pay for his car. I had never committed a crime in my entire life, but I did that night.

I stole the entire deposit from work; $800 in cash, and $2,000 more in checks and credit card slips that we couldn't use. Kevin dissolved the checks and receipts in a bucket of bleach and water, and flushed it down the toilet. We still didn't have enough cash.

My friend Meredith and I were scheduled to work together the next day. While we were talking, she confided in me a secret she had been keeping. She told me that one night when she left work Kevin was outside waiting for her. He had made advances toward her and told her that no one had to know. She totally brushed him off, but felt I needed to know. Had I found out one day sooner, I would never have stolen the money, and Kevin's precious car would have been repossessed.

I was so hurt, I didn't know how to respond. I had always suspected that Kevin was chasing after other women, but this was the first time I had concrete evidence. Of course, he denied it.

The following week, store investigators came to the store while I was working, and the guilt practically consumed me. I simply confessed. I confided in the officer and told him why I did it. The investigator thanked me for being honest. He sympathized with me, but he still pressed charges against me for felony embezzlement.

A week later I was contacted by a police officer and he asked me to come down and deal with the charges. I agreed. And for the first time in my life, I got arrested. I was fingerprinted, took a mug shot, and then I was put in jail with the other criminals.

I was so cooperative that the officers couldn't believe I had really done such a thing. I finally had a chance to tell that officer what was going on in my household. I honestly believed I would get the help I needed and put a stop to what Kevin was doing to me. But I didn't.

Once again I thought about the infamous quote "what goes on behind closed doors, stays behind closed doors. "So I took the heat and figured I could fix my problems at home on my own.

Kevin felt bad and figured the least he could do was try and find me a good attorney. Kevin quickly showed his ugly side to her as well and she only represented me because she could clearly see that he was the mastermind behind the whole scam. On the day of court, Kevin didn't even show up for moral support. His absence gave my attorney even more ammunition to drag his character through the mud. She explained my situation to the judge and got my charges reduced to a misdemeanor larceny.

I received supervised probation and was instructed to pay back the entire amount taken. I was elated with the outcome because in reality, I could have gone to jail.

For obvious reasons, the clothing store fired me. So, I began doing manual labor as a handler at the post office although I was pregnant. I never complained—just showed up at work on time and did my job. Kevin mostly sat home playing with the kids, watching television, and lamenting his condition in life. He hated the fact that I was working in a job he felt was beneath his standards. He hated the fact that I was making money—even if it wasn't a lot—and he wasn't. He hated the fact that everything he had worked for was being taken away.

The bills were still piling up and we didn't have the money to pay. I was arrested again for writing bad checks, and we lost the apartment. When the landlord arrived with the final eviction notice, Kevin was furious. He lost his temper and created such a scene that the landlord called the police and filed charges against him. Kevin was charged with "communicating a threat"—a misdemeanor charge in the penal system.

Inevitably, Kevin took out his anger and frustration on me and on the apartment. When we packed to move, he left 18 full bags of trash in the apartment. The carpet was ruined and the walls needed to be painted. We didn't do any minor repairs or try to leave it in good shape to get back our security deposit. In total, there was more than $5,000 worth of damage to the apartment.

Kevin and I spent all day before I went to work trying to find a new place to live. Both of our credit reports were ruined, so neither of us could get the apartment in our own name. I couldn't take the pressure of being homeless anymore, so without Kevin's approval, I contacted his mother and told her our situation.

With our current financial situation and a third baby on the way, she came down and got us an apartment in her name. Of course, the apartment was beneath Kevin's standards, but we had no choice.

When the maintenance workers or landlord came by, Kevin pretended that he was just visiting his mom so they wouldn't kick us out. Our lives became increasingly complicated and completely constructed out of lies.

His mom begged us to keep up the payments to protect her credit. But we didn't have the money and simply could not afford to pay our bills on time. My car was repossessed shortly after we moved into the apartment.

Once again, Kevin was upset and blamed everything on me.

The holidays were coming up, which were usually good times for us. It was a time when presents were wrapped around the tree and Kevin acted just as happy and excited as the kids. But this particular Christmas was the worst ever. We couldn't afford to get the kids what they wanted, and that just tore Kevin apart. I was just thankful we had somewhere to live; I wasn't in jail and our new baby was on the way.

Two weeks after Christmas, while Kevin was watching football on television, I went into labor. He took me to the hospital and ended up getting into an argument with my physician. The entire time at the hospital was a nightmare and a series of never-ending accusations.

"Whitney, I told you I didn't want any more kids," Kevin said as I walked down the hallway in the labor and delivery section of the hospital. "Are you sure this baby is mine? I don't remember the night we conceived it."

It didn't matter to Kevin that I was trying to have a baby. He was only concerned about the fact that he didn't want any more children. It seemed to me that his timing was a bit off. Through my entire labor and delivery process, Kevin accused me of cheating on him and getting pregnant on purpose. I cried the entire time. The doctors and nurses were sympathetic because they thought I was crying from the pain. However, the physical pain was nothing compared to the mental anguish Kevin caused me that day.

Thad was a healthy baby boy… who looked just like his father.

By the time I went back to work after my son was born, Kevin was still unemployed. I was now routinely writing worthless checks for food to feed my growing family. We were broke and didn't even have enough money for diapers or milk. I worked sporadically at part-time jobs wherever and whenever I could. It felt like 'the Little family against the world.'

Before I completely lost control of my entire life, I decided to have my tubes tied—with or without Kevin's consent. I was only 23, but I had already been through four abortions and given birth to three children. I absolutely did not want any more children with Kevin.

He did not approve. His argument was that if I got my tubes tied, then I could sleep around with other men without him knowing about it. I scheduled an appointment anyway, took the car myself, and went in for a procedure to have my tubes laser sealed. That procedure would prevent me from getting pregnant again.

After the procedure was complete, I couldn't drive myself home, so I called the only person I knew. Meredith picked me up from the hospital, took me home to pick up Kevin and the kids, and brought us back to get our car. This was the first time Kevin had seen her since she accused him of coming on to her. I guess this was Kevin's chance to try and prove to me that it never happened. Kevin called her everything but a child of God. From "whore" to "slut" and things I never heard of—she was it. I kept constantly telling him to stop, but he wouldn't.

He didn't care that the children were in the car either. I don't know who was more embarrassed, Meredith or me, but he didn't let up until we got to the car. Adding insult to injury, he got out of her car, slammed the door and spit on her car. I apologized to Meredith for Kevin's behavior and thanked her for picking me up. She accepted my apology, but I never saw or heard from Meredith again.

I got another job working at a telemarketing and distribution fulfillment company called T.M.S. I was earning less than before, which increased the financial strain and tension even more. Kevin hated the fact that I worked there because a lot of men worked there too. He started accusing me of cheating on him again, and the violence increased.

Almost every month, one or both of us got arrested for bad checks. One night, we were both arrested at the same time, and Kevin's parents had to drive down from Virginia to get the kids and bail us out. Of course, when the officers showed up, Kevin denied ever writing a bad check in his life.

Kevin acted out so badly, that the officers threatened to spray him with pepper spray and called a separate car for him to be booked immediately. I, on the other hand, calmly told the truth and explained the situation to the officer.

Because I had told the truth, instead of the officer calling child protective services to take the children away while their parents went to jail, they allowed me to leave without handcuffs and agreed not to process my arrest until Kevin's parents arrived.

Kevin's parents arrived a few hours later. They didn't say a whole lot, but it was obvious that they were fed up with Kevin and with me. Their precious son— who could do no wrong—was locked up in jail, and I'm sure they thought I was the blame. However, to their credit, they didn't do a lot of finger-pointing. It seems they finally realized that Kevin and I were in a lot of trouble, and so they did what they could to help.

Just when I thought things couldn't get any worse, Kevin's pride and joy got repossessed. It happened around 3:00 in the morning. After hearing the car squealing down the street behind the tow truck, he jumped up. Kevin chased the repo man to the end of the apartment complex trying to retrieve his car. Kevin woke me up and made me sit up with him.

He was so angry he couldn't speak. I just knew he was going to kill me that night because he blamed everything on me. He spent the entire night threatening me and playing games with my mind. It was the fear of the unknown. I secretly wished he would just beat me and get it over with rather than intimidate me and play games with my mind. I became so afraid that my face broke out with small red spots from fear and anxiety.

Once again Kevin's parents came to the rescue and let us borrow one of their used cars. Now Kevin felt he would never live down the fact that his parents had put the apartment in their name, bailed us out of jail, and now given us another car. Kevin couldn't take defeat any longer.

Literally everyday for the next three months, Kevin abused me. For the first time, I knew my life was in jeopardy. Going to work was the thing I most looked forward to because I was safe there. I would smile from the time I left my house to the end of my shift, and then cry all the way home because I knew what was waiting for me. I never let on at work that I was going through hell at home.

My days and nights were filled with torment. I woke up to him kicking me in the rear end or pulling me out of the bed by my hair and dragging me around the house. I went to bed only when he was convinced that he had raped and beaten the truth out of me.

If I came home one minute late, I got a beating. One night, when I got home late from work, Kevin got upset. He screamed profanities at me and locked me out of the house. I was fed up and decided that I was going to leave him. I ran down the stairs, and he chased me outside to the car. I ran back toward the front door, but he caught me and started punching me all over my body. Our fighting became disruptive, so the neighbors called the police. When they arrived, I froze. I never said a word to them about what Kevin had done to me.

As a matter of fact, I lied and covered up for him. I told them it was just a misunderstanding; that I had forgotten my house key, and that everything was fine. I can remember the police officer asking me twice if everything was OK, and I looked him directly in the eyes and said "yes."

If only eyes could talk!

When the police left, he just let me go to sleep. I realized then that Kevin was afraid of the police and afraid to go to jail. I figured that information might be the key to making him change. For so long, I had lived in fear. Now I found something that scared him too.

Kevin didn't like being exposed. And as long as his violent behavior remained a secret, he was safe and only I was in harm's way.

The very next day, I told his parents what he was doing to me. I told them that I was going to leave him because I was afraid for my life. I told them that Kevin needed to seek professional help. They told me they would talk to him, and if the kids and I wanted to come and stay with them we were more than welcome.

I considered letting my parents know, but I quickly changed my mind. Kevin had isolated me so far from them that I couldn't even remember their phone number. He made me believe that they never cared for me anyway—especially my mother and father—so why bother. I felt he was all I had, and no one else would be able to help me anyway. I had always wanted to be different from my mother and grandmother, so I determined not to let them see me fail.

I also confided in a couple of co-workers and supervisors. I told them everything. I told them about the beatings. I told them how he had cut my hair and cut up my clothes. I told them about the holes in my walls and doors due to Kevin's bad temper. Through my experience, I learned that violence thrives in darkness, so I started shedding some light on the situation.

Chapter 5: "Blaming the Victim"

"All right everyone, please help yourself to some refreshments and then take a seat. We've got a lot of information to cover tonight, so I'm eager to get started," Whitney said. The L.I.P.S. support group had gathered for its last weekly meeting of the season.

She continued, "Attention everyone, we have a new member with us tonight. His name is Freddy, and he was referred to us from one of our partner agencies here in town. Before we get started, I'd like for Freddy to introduce himself and tell us a little bit about his situation."

Freddy was a handsome man. He was medium height, muscular and clean-shaven. Karen, one of the women in the group raised her hand and said, "Whitney, I don't mean to be rude, but isn't this group for survivors of domestic violence and abuse? I mean, I can't believe that you're allowing him to be a part of this group. The women in here are trying to heal."

Whitney interrupted, "Karen, I think when you hear what Freddy has to say you'll understand. Freddy, go ahead."

He stood up and slowly looked at each of the women in the room. "Good evening everyone. My name is Freddy, and I'm a survivor of domestic violence. I know when I walked in most of you probably thought I was an abuser, but there really are men out here who are afraid of their partner and what they might do to them; I'm one of them.

I remember when I first met Pat. We were madly in love with each other. And the first year and a half of our relationship was wonderful. I noticed some controlling and jealous tendencies, but I mistook that behavior for love because I was starved for attention. It was nice to have someone who cared about where I had been, or where I was going.

It was nice to know that someone loved me. I grew up in an abusive home, and I saw my father and mother fighting almost every night. For years, that's the way I thought a relationship was supposed to be.

Pat and I went everywhere together and spent as much time as possible together. Then I got a promotion at work that required me to travel and spend more time away from home. At first Pat just made snide comments and general accusations. Then those accusations turned into arguments and fights about whether or not I was having an affair.

I was convinced that Pat and I would be together forever until the first hit occurred. We were arguing about how much time I was spending with my co¬workers. I tried to explain that I was working on a very important project, but that wasn't good enough, and Pat didn't believe me. I don't like to argue, so I turned to walk away. In a split second, Pat had grabbed a lamp and smashed it across my back. I fell to the floor and tried to protect myself from the punches. I'm not very fond of confrontation, so I didn't even try to fight back.

I told myself that it wouldn't happen again, and that it was just a one-time event. But deep down, I knew better. I began to keep my thoughts to myself just to avoid arguing. I didn't want to say anything that might upset Pat. The next time it happened, we were out in public. We had gone to dinner and had a lovely evening together. On the way out of the restaurant, I thanked the maitre d' and tipped the valet driver.

When we got in the car, Pat accused me of flirting and sleeping with the wait staff and valet attendants. I know it sounds ridiculous, but it's true. We argued all the way home, and it ended with me going to the emergency room to get 10 stitches and a sling on my right arm.

Our relationship just grew worse over a period of two years until I couldn't take it anymore. I wasn't happy. I wasn't safe. And I knew I had to get out of the relationship for my own peace of mind.

That's what brings me here tonight. We all hear the statistics about battered and abused women. But I'm living proof that men can be victims and survivors of abuse as well. I know that 93 percent of the victims are women, but that still leaves seven percent. I'd like to thank you for allowing me to share my story and to begin my healing process."

Freddy took his seat and each of the women in the room just sat quietly looking around at each other, not knowing what to say next. Whitney spoke up, "Freddy, thank you so much for coming tonight and for sharing your story. We're very glad that you're here and invite you to come back anytime and continue your healing process."

Karen raised her hand to speak. "Uh, Freddy, I guess I owe you an apology. You're right. I took one look at you and figured you to be the abuser—not the victim. I mean, survivor. I'm sorry that I misjudged you. Please accept my apologies. I really congratulate you on being so courageous and getting yourself out of a bad situation."

Freddy stood up, walked over to Karen and held out his arms for a hug. "There's no need to apologize," he said. "Thank you so much Karen." She stood up and the two embraced each other. Indeed, the healing process had already begun.

Whitney passed around a flyer to each individual. "Tonight, we're going to learn about some of the most common misconceptions about battery and domestic violence." The flyer listed the following information:

Misconception 1: The problem is spouse abuse; couples who assault each other.

In reality, 93% of serious assaults are against women. Battering is a relationship in which one person coerces, intimidates and dominates another, and women are its principal victims.

Misconception 2: Drugs and alcohol cause violence.

Addictions are used as excuses to free the batterer from responsibility for the behavior, i.e. "the drugs made me do it." This theory does not explain why the batterer uses violence or why he batters when sober. The addictive batterer must be treated for two separate problems—the addiction and the violence.

Misconception 3: Stress causes battering.

Obviously some batterers experience stress, but stress does not cause abuse. Many men under severe stress do not batter. Even if a batterer reduces stress, the violence will continue or resume because the batterer still feels entitled to assault his partner. Violence itself must be treated as the problem, not as a symptom that will disappear.

Misconception 4: Battered women are masochistic and provoke the violence.

Battered women are not a personality type. Any woman can find herself in a potentially violent situation. Abused women do not enjoy the beatings, nor do most women feel they deserve the assault. "Provocation" is a concept that blames the victim and frees the abuser of responsibility for the violence. Women are NOT responsible for their abusers' behavior.

Misconception 5: Battered women do not seek help nor will they use it once it is offered.

Most battered women make many efforts to stop the violence or to seek help from agencies in their community. Unfortunately, they are often met with misunderstanding and responses that encourage them to reunite with the abuser or ignore the abuse. As a result, many women are reluctant to ask for assistance.

However, when greeted with empathy and genuine concern, many battered women are willing to reach out for help and courageously share their experiences.

Misconception 6: "Battering" overstates the case; few women are actually beaten.

Once violence has begun in a relationship, it will continue and will increase in frequency and severity. Battering can involve severe beatings or threats, rape, weapons and mental or physical torture.

Misconception 7: Battering is a family matter.

Assault is a crime in all 50 states. Battering is not simply a family problem, but also a far-reaching social problem affecting as many as 50% of all U.S. women. Violence against wives will occur at least once in 2/3 of all marriages and at least 25% of wives in the U.S. are severely beaten during their marriages. More than one million abused women seek medical help for injuries caused by battering each year. Battering is the number one cause of emergency room visits by women.

Misconception 8: Only low-income, working class families experience violence.

Battering affects all racial, social, ethnic, economic and religious groups and affects each group with equal frequency. Battered women with few resources are more visible because they seek help from public agencies.

Misconception 9: Battered women are a particular and easily definable group of women.

Battered women are as diverse as women are. There is no particular kind of woman who is likely to be battered any more than there is any kind of woman who is likely to be raped. The only "kind" of woman who is battered is the woman who finds herself with a partner who batters.

Misconception 10: The violence can't be that bad, or she wouldn't stay with him.

In the U.S. today, on the average, a woman earns slightly more than half of what a man earns. For this reason, many women—including battered women—do not feel that they can support themselves and their children. Fear of retaliation for leaving, harassment and further violence from the abuser are also traps for battered women. Statistically, the most dangerous time for a battered woman is when she is leaving or her abuser believes she is leaving.

That night, the individuals in the group discussed the information they had learned and talked about ways to educate the public about the seriousness of domestic violence and domestic abuse. As Whitney was packing up her things, she thought about how many people had blamed her for the situation with Kevin and how many people had misunderstood her predicament.

She knew that as long as people could blame the victim and make up reasons to blame the woman for her abuser's behavior, then they didn't have to accept the reality of violence in families across the country. It was easy to stereotype and label women who had no identity, but she was determined to give domestic violence a name and a face. The world couldn't ignore this issue forever.

The drive home that night seemed longer than usual. Whitney looked in her rearview mirror and noticed a car following closely behind her. She made a quick right turn onto a side street in her neighborhood, and the other vehicle turned right in behind her.

She sped up and maneuvered her car back onto a main thoroughfare, but the car behind her was in hot pursuit. When she slowed down, the other car slowed down as well. When she sped up, the other car sped up as well. Whitney slammed on the brakes, and the car behind her swerved and sped past her. She looked up just in time to see a car full of giggling and rowdy teenagers out joyriding. She nervously began the trip back to her home and spent most of the time looking in the mirror waiting for her would-be assailant to appear.

Whitney drove around the block twice to make sure no one was following her or hiding outside her apartment building before she finally felt comfortable enough to get out of the car and go inside. By the time she got home, her children were already tucked in bed and fast asleep. She paid the babysitter and then double-checked all the doors and windows to make sure they were locked.

Tossing and turning, the same recurring nightmare that haunted her dreams disrupted her sleep. There was never a face, only a shadowy figure that hid in corners and behind doors waiting to attack.

Even as she slept, she could feel his warm breath against her skin and his hands gripped tightly around her throat. She struggled against him, kicking her legs and swinging her arms in the air.

She gasped to take another breath before her lungs collapsed. Whitney sat up in bed and grabbed the knife that she kept hidden under the mattress. She wiped the dripping sweat from her forehead and sat silently waiting to see if it was only a dream. It was. Her bedroom was quiet—aside from the sound of her own heartbeat echoing inside her chest.

A glass of warm milk and some soothing music on the radio helped her drift off to sleep. When she woke up in the morning, her face, neck and body was covered in hives. It was one of many symptoms caused by stress and the fear of abuse she had endured for so long. She looked in the mirror and realized that she hardly recognized herself.

She opened the front door, looked around and picked up the morning newspaper. That's how she started each day. She always read the front-page headlines first, then the comics and then the horoscopes to see what the future held. She read the obituaries last.

Every few months, there was a familiar face. It was that of another victim of domestic violence who simply did not get out in time. Several of the faces belonged to women who had attended L.I.P.S. and then returned to the abusive environment.

Today's paper featured an older woman who had been killed several years ago. It was the same photo and write-up that ran every year on this date. Each year, the woman's family ran a memorial ad and picture in tribute to her memory. Underneath the photo caption, it read: "To our beloved daughter, sister and friend. Though you are no longer with us, your memory lives on forever."

Whitney just stared at the woman in the picture for a while, and a single tear rolled down her face and dropped onto the paper. This face was not only familiar, it was family.

Her aunt Lena had been an indirect victim of domestic violence before the situation escalated out of control. Lena's daughter dated an abuser, and as a result, the entire family suffered with her as she struggled to survive the uncertainties of an abusive relationship.

On a fateful day, the abusive boyfriend and Lena's daughter had a fight, and he vowed to kill her if she tried to leave him again. She left anyway, and he followed her back to her mother's house. Lena was in the kitchen preparing dinner, and her other daughter was on the back porch. He jumped out of the car after her as she ran inside the front door and out the back door.

The boyfriend saw Lena in the kitchen, yelled at her and shot her point blank. She slumped over and fell on the kitchen table, and was dead before she hit the floor. Hearing the gunshot ring out, Lena's daughter kept running into the woods behind the house.

The boyfriend continued in pursuit of her and encountered her sister on the back porch. He shot her as well. Although the injury was life threatening, fortunately, she pulled through. He was arrested and sentenced to 50 years in prison. But no matter how swift or severe the punishment, it still didn't bring Lena back to her family.

The next two hours of Whitney's morning were filled with the typical activities of getting the kids ready for school and daycare. Whitney was scheduled to speak on domestic violence to a group of 500 teenagers at one of the local high schools. Younger audiences were always challenging, so she spent some extra time going over her speech.

By the time Whitney got up to speak, the students seemed restless and weary of hearing about domestic violence warning signs and statistics. So she chose a different approach. She told her story—detailing the intimate details of how her ex-husband had terrorized her for more than a decade. She told them how he had fractured her nose and left scars and bruises all over her body. She shared with them how many times he had raped her and how he had stalked her and threatened her life.

At the end of her presentation, she had everyone's complete attention. In those 30 minutes, domestic violence had become real to those students. Whitney hoped that her talk would help some young person avoid becoming a victim. During the question and answer period, one student raised her hand.

"Yes, what is your name," Whitney asked.

"I'm Beverly, and I wanted to ask you a question about some of the things you went through with your ex-husband."

"OK. I don't mind answering your questions, because you never know, your question might help save somebody's life," Whitney said.

Beverly got a real serious look on her face and said, "If you knew that your ex-husband was wrong for beating you, and you knew that writing bad checks was illegal, why did you stay with him, and why did you go along with his plan and steal money from other people?"

"That's an excellent question Beverly, and I'm going to answer it as truthfully as I can," Whitney said.

"One of the most popular questions people ask about domestic violence is 'why do women stay with men who abuse them?' But I must tell you that no one falls in love with an abuser, because that's not the part of the personality that you initially meet. I fell in love with a wonderful young man who loved me. But by the time the abuse became evident, I had already invested a lot of energy and emotion into our relationship.

"Even after a fight, Kevin would always apologize and tell me how much he loved me. I really wanted to believe that it was true, because I loved him too. There are a lot of reasons for why some women stay. They include love, fear, children, economics, guilt, shame, low self-esteem, denial, embarrassment, religion and commitment. Those are all major issues to address, and it's not easy to start over. Sometimes, you have to make hard choices.

"Yes, I knew stealing was wrong. But by that time, we had children, and we were desperate. Kevin was unemployed, and my salary wasn't enough to support our household. I made some tough choices and some wrong decisions. I admit that. But I also did what I thought was necessary to stay safe and to stay alive. In a domestic violence situation, it's all about survival, and you do what you have to do.

"I wrote the checks to feed my family. And I wrote them because Kevin threatened to beat me if I didn't do what he said. When I was your age—or maybe even younger—I vowed to do anything and everything I could to keep my family together.

"I didn't want my kids to grow up without a father, so I was determined to do whatever I had to do to make the relationship work. Honestly, Beverly... fear and desperation will make you do things you never dreamed you would do. During that time, I became someone I didn't even recognize. I wrote bad checks, I stole money from my job, and I became very familiar with the criminal justice system."

Whitney had captured the attention of her teenage audience, and they sat and listened attentively. Maybe if young people could understand some of the circumstances of abuse and violence early, they could avoid the consequences later.

She continued, "It seems like it would be so easy to just pack up and leave a dangerous situation, but in reality, the situation gets more dangerous when you try to leave. As a matter of fact, that's the time when most domestic violence murders are committed. At the time, I had no family nearby and nowhere else to go. In addition, I had small children and was pregnant with my son at the time. Imagine having to start over, support a family and escape from an abusive spouse—without any support." Beverly nodded her head and took a seat back amongst her classmates.

Next, a young man walked up to the microphone in the auditorium to ask a question. "Ms. Little, I have a question for you. If I heard you right, you said that your husband—I mean, your ex-husband—went to prison for kidnapping, sexually assaulting and raping you. I don't mean any disrespect, but how can a husband rape his own wife?" There were nods and whispering in the audience. Obviously it was a question that struck a nerve with the students.

Whitney saw this as an excellent opportunity to educate the students about the different forms of abuse and how the controlling personality of an abuser justified certain actions and behavior.

"What is your name," she asked.

"My name is Mitch."

"Well Mitch, there are a lot of people—including professionals who worked on my case—who asked the same question. The thing most people don't understand about rape is that it's a crime about power, control and domination. It's not just about sex. In actuality, sex is the weapon that's used to exert that power and control.

"And regardless of whether a couple is married or not, if a husband forces his wife to have sex, it's still considered rape. Being married doesn't give either one of the spouses a license to abuse their partner. Marriage is an institution built on love and respect.

"Rape is a crime. And so when my ex-husband abused me and forced me to have sex with him, he was trying to dominate and control the power in our relationship. He wasn't demonstrating love. So yes, a woman has a right to be safe in her marriage just like a husband does. And it is possible for a man to rape his own wife. And it is also justice for him to be punished for it."

Mitch sat back down with a puzzled look on his face. It was obvious he was not convinced by Whitney's response.

Another young lady came up to the microphone. "Ma'am, I just want to thank you for telling your story. I don't think a lot of people realize how serious this really is, and I have a friend that I think may be in a potentially dangerous situation. I'm not sure how to approach the subject because I don't want her to get mad at me and think I'm trying to get in her business.

"But anyway, my question for you is, 'Why didn't your ex-husband get a job?' It seems like he beat you and then made you support the family too. Why didn't you make him go to work and help take care of his responsibilities?"

Whitney shook her head as she thought back to remember the situation. "Kevin had such a bad temper and unstable personality, that he couldn't keep a job for more than four or five months. Although he was intelligent and talented, he couldn't get along with his co-workers and supervisors. And in the real world, you can get fired for having a bad attitude. I kept working because I knew that one of us had to provide and put food on the table for our kids.

"Kevin resented me for working and getting a job when he couldn't. He resented the fact that people seemed to be on my side—and not his. And he still blamed me for destroying his dreams and ruining his basketball career. He had a lot of anger, and he took that out on me in a lot of different ways.

"The ways were not just physical and sexual abuse, but also mental, financial and verbal abuse. The worse things got, the more depressed he became, and he just gave up all together. Eventually, he stopped looking for a job completely and started creating different ways to get something for nothing. He would complain at restaurants to get his meals for free. I slipped and fell in a restaurant while carrying my third child; he made money off of that. He even used his parents' social security numbers to open up a credit card account without their knowledge. This definitely wasn't the young man that I had fallen in love with.

"Honestly, I couldn't make Kevin do anything. At the time, he had all the control and power in our relationship. I wanted him to go to work, and I needed him to go to work. I wanted a normal life. But I also knew that if I didn't go to work, then I would have to stay home and suffer even more abuse from him. Even though he was beating me every day, I knew that I was not responsible for his behavior. Even if Kevin wouldn't do the right thing, I had to."

The students were captivated by the information Whitney shared and seemed to genuinely appreciate what she was trying to teach them. She hoped that they would share with others the things they had learned today.

"We have time for one more question," Whitney said.

Another young lady stood up and came to the microphone. "Hello, Miss Little. My name is Miracle. My mother named me that because she was pregnant with me when her boyfriend almost beat her to death. I'd like to know why you didn't just call the police the first time your ex-husband hit you, or why you didn't tell the truth when your neighbors called the police."

Whitney paused for a moment before she answered, "Miracle, thank you for asking that question. In my case, I didn't call the police because I knew it would only make things worse. Kevin hated for other people to know "our business," and he definitely didn't want me getting outsiders involved in what he considered our personal lives. At that time, I thought the punishment for domestic violence was not severe enough to protect me from him. And I also had nowhere to go with small children. I knew that if I left, and Kevin found me, that he'd probably kill me."

Whitney looked at her watch and said, "I see that we're out of time. I just want to thank you all for being so attentive and for asking such great questions. I hope that something I've said here today was helpful." She received a standing ovation.

Whitney's story was a familiar one, and it resonated with women of all ages and backgrounds all over the world. Because of her experiences, she vowed to make a difference and to tell her story to anyone that would listen:

Domestic violence was so common in our home that our kids—and even the neighbors—got used to it. At first, the children would scream and cry and try to help me. After a while, they stopped crying, they stopped trying to help, and eventually they would just sit through it and watch cartoons without blinking an eye. I remember asking myself, 'what message am I sending to my kids?'

Because we were a family, Kevin became very comfortable in the relationship and figured that I would stay with him because of the kids. His obsessive-compulsive behavior became more evident, and other signs of his personality disorder began to emerge. If we all went somewhere together, he would spend five minutes just opening and closing the door to make sure it was shut. After dinner, Kevin would hit each eye of the stove to make sure they were off; then he'd turn the knobs on and off—just to make sure. At night before bed, he would lock and unlock the door over and over again. Then he would pace across the living room floor, mumble to himself, and start the process all over again.

I had seen telltale signs of this behavior when we were in high school, but not at this magnitude. He became even more possessive and turned into a pack rat. He kept old high school and college papers, receipts, candy wrappers, and coupons. He wouldn't throw anything away, and he didn't want anybody to touch his belongings. He became very junky and refused to help keep our apartment clean. At the time, I had no explanation for his behavior. I begged him to go to counseling, but he refused to seek help.

The fighting began to intensify, and we even began fighting with the kids in the room. Kevin started teaching the kids to disrespect me, even though I was their mother.

One afternoon, he actually told the children not to call me "mommy" anymore.

My oldest daughter was five; my sons were three years and nine months old. When I got home from work, they ran to meet me at the front door, yelling out, "Mommy, mommy, we missed you!" Kevin was enraged. He threw a glass against the wall and said, "You don't call her mommy. She's a whore and a slut. That's what you call her!" The kids just stared at him blankly and hugged me tighter. I was too afraid to say anything because I knew that would only start another fight, and I didn't want the kids to get involved.

There was a defining moment in my life when I knew that things had to change, or the damage would be irreversible. My oldest son was standing in a chair at the kitchen sink playing in the water. I told him, "Honey, get down from there. I don't want you to fall."

"I don't want to. Leave me alone," he screamed at the top of his lungs.

"Excuse me? Mommy said 'get down.'"

"No! I don't have to. Leave me alone, or I'm going to tell daddy to take you into that room again, and beat you." It was official… we had now taught our three-year-old that it was OK for a man to beat a woman. And if he had picked up on that at the age of three, then I knew my daughter had gotten the same message. Something had to change. But things got worse before they got better.

I looked horrible and I felt horrible. My self-esteem was at its lowest point. If my check was a penny short, I got a beating. I couldn't afford new clothes or pay to get my hair done. If Kevin didn't like something I was wearing, he would rip or cut my clothes right off of my body and destroy them.

After a while, I only had a total of five outfits, two bras and one pair of shoes. When I took it upon myself to purchase a new pair of shoes because the heel was coming off one of them, Kevin took the shoes, put them in the toilet and urinated on them. I didn't even have my own underwear; I had to wear his. He figured that no man would want to have sex with me if I was wearing men's underwear.

The effects of abuse were evident. My speech began to be slurred, and my vision began fading. I had been beaten in the head so many times, I thought I might have some permanent brain damage. Kevin would slap me so hard that I would literally see stars and my ears would ring.

There were cuts and bruises all over my back and legs. I had a golf-ball size knot on my leg from where he kicked me. There were days that I could barely walk because of the abuse. Sometimes the beatings were so severe, I began to have out-of-body experiences.

Over time, Kevin's rage was coupled with paranoia. He would constantly call me at work—every hour of every day. He interrogated me about my work schedule and whom I had talked to that day. He even began examining my body when I got home to make sure I hadn't had sex with another man. It was so humiliating. Then he'd hit me again and force me to have sex.

This would go on until 2:00 or 3:00 in the morning. Then, I'd have to get up, put up with his abuse, go back to work, come home, and it would start all over again.

I was now suffering from physical, financial, verbal, sexual and emotional abuse. Of everything, the mental abuse was the worse, because I never knew what was about to happen next. I lived in a constant state of fear. If we were at home, I couldn't move unless Kevin told me to move. I couldn't go anywhere without his permission. I couldn't go to the bathroom or pick up the crying baby unless he said it was OK.

I started developing a plan to get away. After 10 years with Kevin, I simply couldn't take it anymore. I didn't want to risk leaving and having to come back home. When I finally got up the courage and resources to leave, I did not intend to come back or to look back— ever.

For weeks, I developed my plan to get away from Kevin. I finally reached out to my family and reconnected with my mother and grandmother. They agreed to help me when I was ready to leave and not return.

My mom was moving back to North Carolina and my lease was up, so we had planned to move in together. We would stay with my grandmother in Virginia until we were ready to move. I started to pray again— something I hadn't done in years. We had never attended church as a family, but I knew that God was real. I was desperate, and I needed some help.

I knew that God was the only One who could get me safely out of this situation. The irony is that God loved me unconditionally all along, but I felt too guilty to ask Him for help. I had spent my entire life trying to do the right thing, but because of Kevin, I now felt unworthy to receive or deserve help from God. How could God possibly help me or still love me after all the things I had done? But it didn't matter, because He was still there gently loving me and guiding me to safety.

Looking back, I realize I invested more than 10 years in a relationship that would inevitably kill me if I didn't get out of it. No one told me how costly the price of love could be, but I paid dearly, and so did my children.

When I met Kevin, I had a bright and promising future ahead of me. The sky was the limit. Now after being in a relationship with him, I had low self-esteem, scars and bruises all over my body, a criminal record, and nothing to call my own. I had three beautiful children, but when I thought about the circumstances under which they came into this world, it only depressed me more.

It's hard to walk away from someone you love, but Kevin had evolved into someone I didn't even know. He had beaten me mercilessly, he even went so far as to spit in my face, which stripped me of my dignity—but admittedly—I still loved him. Love is a powerful emotion, and it makes people do irrational and unimaginable things. In my case, it made me give up who I was and settle for less than I deserved in life. Love made me give up my dreams and give away part of my future.

The price of love with Kevin almost cost me everything I had.

I had tried to love Kevin and make things work between us for 10 years. The situation was completely out of control, and so was he. I finally made up my mind it was time to leave. Every week, I took my lunch money and put it aside for my escape. I reached out to others so I could get some help. The most important lesson I learned about getting out is: "Leaving is a process, not an event."

In all the years we had been together, I was completely faithful to Kevin even though he constantly questioned my fidelity. Two weeks before I left Kevin, I met someone else. I'm not proud of what I did, but I had a one-night stand. For the first and only time, I was unfaithful in my marriage.

There was nothing romantic or exciting about it. Meeting this guy was a chance encounter fueled by passion and frustration. I don't even remember his name. He saw me at the drugstore as I was walking back to my car, and asked me my name. He complimented me and said he'd like to get to know me better. He was just there when I needed someone to care.

We arranged to meet later that night. I knew Kevin had my schedule memorized, so I did some of my errands early to free up some time that evening. I went to the guy's apartment, and we spent 15 minutes together—no more, no less. There were no flowers or candlelight dinner, just two people who were starved for attention. I left without saying a word.

When I got home that night, Kevin made me strip so he could examine me again. As usual, we fought; he beat me and then forced me to have sex. It's interesting how I had been wrongly accused of infidelity for years, and still got beat. And on that night, I looked him in the eyes and lied with that same straight face; and got a beating. As I was falling asleep that night I waited for the guilt of my infidelity to kick in. It never did. For me, the lack of guilt or concern was confirmation that my relationship with Kevin was over, and it was time to leave him and get on with my life.

Friday, September 17, 1998 is a day I will never forget. The previous night I had to convince Kevin that a co-worker was willing to fix my hair for me. Kevin wasn't concerned about my appearance at work; he just didn't want me to look too good for my male co-workers. The hairdo was free, so I didn't think Kevin would mind. Surprisingly, it started an argument, but I won out. I got my hair done.

I admit it took four hour to complete, but it was well worth it. For the first time in years, I felt pretty again. The whole ride home I blocked out the thought of my ugly battered body hiding under my clothes. Before going home I stopped by the grocery store to pick up corndogs and French fries for dinner, still feeling on cloud nine.

When I walked in the door, Kevin immediately lit into me for getting home late and he punched me in my head and back. I slumped over and fell to the floor. Then he grabbed me by my hair and pulled me up. I was kicking and screaming, trying to get away from him. Patches of my hair were on the floor where he had pulled it out by the roots. He called me every name imaginable, and then threw a cup of water in my face and hair. My three children were standing at the bedroom door watching.

Kevin told the kids to come over and laugh at "mommy's ugly new hairdo that was all wet." The three of them pointed and laughed at me like bullies on a school playground. I just stood there in shock. Kevin stated that he didn't want "that crap" that I brought home for dinner either and that I needed to take it back. I agreed and walked out the door. He didn't even realize I didn't take the bag of groceries with me.

I know God was with me that day because when I left, I didn't look back. I got in the car, went across the street to a pay phone, and called my supervisor. I told her what had happened, that I was leaving Kevin and going to the police. The whole trip to the police station I was waiting for that little voice to tell me to turn around and go back home. But I never heard it.

When I arrived at the station a female and male officer greeted me. I had explained in detail the horror I was living in at home and that I had had enough. I told them I just wanted them to escort me home to get my children and some of my belongings. I didn't want to press charges against Kevin—I just wanted it all to end peacefully.

The police officers filed a report and took pictures of my battered body. They begged me to press charges but I kept saying no. The officers then ran a background check on Kevin and found an outstanding warrant for another worthless check, so they picked him up immediately. I didn't want him to get arrested, but it was no longer my decision.

The two officers followed me back to the apartment. When we got there I stayed in the car until they had Kevin in custody. When the officer went to the door, Kevin wouldn't answer, so he came and got my key to let himself in. All of the lights were off in the apartment and Kevin stated he didn't hear the door because he was giving the children a bath. Kevin was finally arrested and taken to jail.

He had to stay in jail for 48 hours before his parents could bail him out. Once Kevin was released, he moved in with his parents. The children and I went back to Virginia with my mother and my grandmother.

The court hearing set a lot of things into motion. A protective restraining order was established that forced Kevin to stay away from me. Kevin was no longer able to write or communicate with me by telephone, and he was required to stay at least 100 yards away from me. The judge had given me full custody of the children, which gave me control over when he could see them. I was awarded the apartment until the lease was up even though I didn't stay there. Kevin's parents couldn't take the car away from me nor take the insurance off due to the fact that I was still working to provide for the children.

The judge ordered Kevin to go to counseling. Finally someone listened to me and realized he needed to get some help. When we walked out of the courtroom, I felt a sense of relief, but Kevin was determined to initiate the same cycle over again. I remember him following me out of the courtroom and screaming out my name. "Whitney, Whitney, I love you. I'm so sorry. Please come back to me and let's try to work things out. Please don't leave me! I'm sorry. Whitney!" He followed me onto the elevator and out to the car. We hadn't even left the courthouse, and he was already violating the protective order I had against him.

"Whitney," he cried. "I can't believe you're going to tear our family apart. What about the kids? You said you loved me. I love you, Whitney. Please take me back. Please don't leave me. I'll go to counseling. I'll get help. I'll do whatever you want me to do—just please don't leave me. I was wrong. I was in jail—for god's sake—please don't do this to me. Please!"

I didn't want a scene, and I didn't want to start an argument. So I just tried to placate him. I spoke very softly, "Kevin, I'll always love you, but you've gone too far. I can't keep living like this."

He interrupted me, "I know. I know. I was wrong, and I'm sorry. I'll get help. Please help me… just don't leave me. Don't tear our family apart like this. Just give me another chance. Please Whitney, just give me another chance."

"Kevin, it's over. You had your chances, and you refused to get help. I will always love you, but it's time for us to move on." Although I had custody of the kids, I still let them stay with Kevin. Since I was still working and Kevin wasn't, he kept the kids during the week and I got them on the weekends. Even if we couldn't stay married, I thought he should have a relationship with his children. I wanted them to know their father.

I really wanted to help Kevin, and I wanted him to get the psychological help that he needed—not so we could be together again—but so he could have a productive future. Since both of his parents worked during the day and refused to give him the money to attend counseling, the psychologist wouldn't accept him as a patient. Kevin begged and pleaded with me to help him, so I did. Against my better judgment, I agreed to pay for his counseling and take him to a domestic violence education program as part of his rehabilitation.

Unfortunately, we arrived late. I had to pay a fine, and he never went back. He still wasn't ready to accept responsibility for his actions.

Now that Kevin and the kids were living with his parents, he was catching hell on a daily basis. A day didn't go by without being reminded of his failure as a husband and a father. There was so much conflict in the house that Kevin was afraid to say or do anything. He constantly called and begged me to come back to him. The answer was always "no," but that didn't stop him from trying.

Now that Kevin was out of the picture, I tried to begin piecing my life back together. I found a new sense of strength. I found a new sense of purpose. I found a new sense of self. I vowed to myself that I would no longer be a victim. Even though I was angry about how Kevin had treated me, and how he had destroyed our family, I never spoke negatively about him in front of our children. He was still their father, and they loved him.

I was still carrying out my plan to get my own place for the kids and me. By staying with my grandmother, I was able to save a lot of money. I worked as much overtime as I could. I was planning to start a new life with the children—free from fear.

One day while I was working, a new training class rolled out. For the first time in a while, a man caught my eye.

After what I had experienced with Kevin, meeting someone new was the furthest thing from my mind. I later found out that he had an interest in me as well. His name was Kell, and he also was going to be working the evening shift at T.M.S.

A co-worker of ours was having a party and Kell asked me to meet him there. At first I was a little hesitant but decided to go. We met later that evening after the party and ended up talking for hours. Kell had a terrific sense of humor, and it felt like we had known each other for years. We became friends immediately.

I told him what I was going through with Kevin. Honestly, I was prepared for him to leave because I figured he wouldn't want to be involved with someone with the kind of emotional baggage I had. But he understood completely, and he even offered to help me get back on my feet. He adored my children, and that meant the world to me.

Kell was the first guy I had dated since I was 14. Dating was completely new to me, because I had spent the past 10 years with Kevin. Kell would call me every morning to say hello and every night to make sure I had gotten home from work safely. It felt nice to be cared for. We spent a lot of time together going to the movies, dinner or just sitting around getting to know each other better.

Kell was showing me how a healthy relationship should be; a relationship without fear or abuse.

It appeared that our lives were about to get back to normal. For the sake of the kids, Kevin and I decided to try and have a family outing together—just like old times. By no means did this mean I was going back to Kevin. I always felt that even though we weren't together, we could still be civil and raise our children. Kell understood that I was trying to maintain a relationship between my children and their father, and he didn't seem to mind.

The agreement was for Kevin and me to meet at his parents' house, and then take the kids to Playworld and dinner. This seemed harmless and would go a long way to help the kids in their healing process. When I first arrived, nervous energy filled the room.

Nobody knew what to say to me, so they focused all their attention on the kids. Kevin motioned toward the door and said that we should get going. The children were excited to have their parents back together again.

We got in the car and Kevin backed out of his parents' driveway. He looked at me and said, "Why do you look so happy without me?" He raised his arm in the air, and the backside of his hand connected with my face. We had only been alone for two minutes, and the abuse had started up again. He reached under my skirt, ripped off my panties and hit me again.

Kevin yelled, "Why are you wearing that dress? Who are you sleeping with? I know you're seeing somebody else. Who is it?" The kids were crying and screaming in the backseat. I put my arm up and tried to protect myself, which only made matters worse.

Kevin drove out of his parents' neighborhood and pulled off on the side of the road. He beat me up in the front seat while our children watched helplessly from the back of the car. Kevin wanted me to know that he was still in control. I begged him to take me back to his parents' house, but he wouldn't listen. So we took the hour and a half drive to the outing. I always carried extra clothes in the trunk, so he allowed me to change before we got out of the car.

The whole time at Playworld and all through dinner, Kevin acted as if nothing out of the ordinary had happened. The kids were laughing and playing, and I just sat quietly and didn't say a word the entire time. I was so angry and so hurt. He was trying to steal back my newfound independence. He was trying to make me powerless again.

Kevin had violated every requirement in the court's protective order and realized that I could send him back to jail. The conversation the rest of the evening was one-sided with him begging me not to file charges against him. "Whitney, please don't call the police," he said. "Please don't make me go back to jail. I don't belong in jail. When I saw you in that dress, I just lost control. I thought you were dressing up for some other man. I didn't mean to hit you. I won't do it again. Please just don't send me back to jail." I didn't say a word—I just nodded. I just wanted to make it through the evening alive and get back home safely.

When I got home that night, I told my mother everything that had happened, and she immediately called Kevin's father. He apologized too and asked us not to call the police and have Kevin sent back to jail.

My mother and grandmother and I discussed the situation, and I told them that Kevin needed psychological help. I didn't think he would get the help he needed in jail, so I decided not to turn him in. Once again, he didn't have to accept responsibility for his actions. I just stayed as far away from him as I could.

One of our family traditions was to go to the circus together every year in October. This year would be no different, even though we were no longer a family. I told the kids that the circus was in town, and that I had already purchased our tickets. My daughter asked, "Is daddy coming too?" I was silent for a moment. The kids cried and pleaded with me to invite their dad to the circus. "Daddy always goes to the circus with us. If daddy doesn't go, I don't want to go either." I called Kevin and told him about the circus.

To prevent a repeat of our family Playworld and dinner outing, I took my younger sister and brother to the circus with us. I thought this extra measure of precaution would protect me from Kevin's abuse. It didn't.

While the kids were playing and enjoying the attractions, Kevin started up again. "Whitney, please come back to me. Please take me back." I couldn't even enjoy the circus because Kevin talked the entire time— begging me to come back to him.

"Whitney, did you hear me? Are you listening to me? Please don't leave me. Please take me back." He went on and on and on. If I had a penny for every time Kevin called my name, I would have become a millionaire in a day. By the time the circus was over, I was exhausted.

As we all headed back to the car after the circus, I bumped into two male co-workers from my job at T.M.S. carrying a huge stuffed teddy bear. I waved at them and said, "Hey guys! How are you? Is that teddy bear for me? I'll see you at work on Monday." They smiled and walked past us.

The very next moment, I felt Kevin's fist pounding into my back. The force with which he hit me bruised the back of my ribs and caused my back to swell. He grabbed me by my arm and squeezed it so tightly I thought he was going to break it. "Who the hell was that? I knew you were sleeping with somebody else. Are you sleeping with both of them? Answer me!" I tried to snatch my arm out of his grasp. He grabbed me tighter and practically dragged me the rest of the way to the car. The whole time, he was saying, "I knew it. I knew you were messing around."

When we got to the car, Kevin slammed me into the side of it and said, "That's it. I'm putting an end to this. I'm going to kill you tonight. Do you hear me? Tonight, I'm gonna kill you!" My brother, sister and children were all standing a few feet away watching. I honestly didn't think he'd do anything with that many witnesses. I didn't take him seriously, so I said to my sister, "You heard him right? So if I end up dead, you know he did it."

On the way home, around 11:00 p.m., I told Kevin to stop at an all-night convenience store so that I could buy diapers for the baby before heading back to Virginia. My sister, brother and children had fallen asleep in the backseat. I got out and Kevin stayed in the car.

When I walked out of the store, Kevin was waiting for me outside the door. He grabbed me by my arm and said,

"Come with me." There wasn't a lot of traffic at that time of night, so I couldn't call for help. He grabbed me by my arm and shoved me around the corner to the back of the building. "Take off your clothes, Whitney. You know what I want."

"Are you crazy? The kids are in the car! We're not together anymore. I'm not doing that," I said.

"Whitney, I'm not playing games with you, and we're not leaving until you give me what I want. Now take off your clothes." I tried to run away and get back to the car, but he overpowered me and dragged me back behind the building. Kevin was determined to control me, no matter what he had to do. He didn't care about me. He didn't care about going back to jail. He didn't care about getting caught. He just wanted me to know that he was in control of the situation.

I tried to get away again, but he wouldn't let go. After going back and forth with him for several more minutes, I finally gave in. I pulled down my pants and he raped me behind the store. I cried all the way back to the car.

Kevin knew he was going back to jail. So he drove all night long so that I couldn't report him to the police. He was driving and yelling at me—blaming me for making him so angry. Then he would mumble to himself about how out of control the situation was and how he just wanted us to be a family again. By 1:30 that morning, the kids were still asleep, but my sister and brother were demanding to go home.

Kevin knew he was in trouble so he couldn't decide whether to drop himself and the kids off first or me and my siblings. He drove 20 minutes to his parents' house, pulled up in the driveway and then took off again. Then he went to my grandmother's house and did the same thing. Kevin made these trips back and forth three more times. Finally he decided to go back over the North Carolina border and drop us off at an out-of-the-way truck stop.

As my siblings and I were getting out of the car I saw Kevin get out also and come around to my door. He ordered me to get back into the car, but I said no. A truck driver came over and was trying to calm him down. Kevin told him to mind his business and forced me in the car. Leaving my sister and brother behind, Kevin sped off down the highway with the kids and me.

As soon as we left, my sister called our mom, who then called the police. There was a statewide search for our vehicle, and my mom told the police Kevin had kidnapped me. Kevin called his parents, and they informed him that the police were looking for us. He convinced his parents to call the police and tell them everything was OK—and that I had willingly gone with him. They never talked to me. They just called the police and told them that everything was fine. They called off the search.

Kevin drove all night and begged me to come back to him the entire time. Deep down, I felt sorry for Kevin, but it was evident that he had lost control. Slowly but surely, he was losing everything. Kevin was telling me how his life had fallen apart since I left him. The whole time I was listening but also thinking of ways to get him to return me home safely.

After riding around until 6:00 in the morning, I convinced Kevin to go home. I told him that I would attend counseling with him and maybe we could get our family back together. I took him and the children to his parents' house and I finally got away with my life—again.

When I got to my grandmother's house, my mother lit into me. She thought that the story his parents told her was true. I explained the truth, and once again she got on the phone with his parents. Mr. Little (again) begged my mother not to press charges even though this time Kevin also endangered my brother, sister and children. Once again we decided not to involve the police. It was very clear to us that Kevin needed help—not jail.

Even with all of the chances I had given Kevin to avoid jail, he still wouldn't let up. He called me at work one day and told me that baby was sick and that I needed to come right away to take him to the hospital. Kevin's plan was to get me over to his parents' house while no one else was there. Little did he know, I was coming with my mother and grandmother. Kevin stayed home while we took the baby to the emergency room. There was absolutely nothing wrong with the baby.

Just when I thought he had finally gotten the message, he surprised me once more. One Saturday while Kevin and his parents were home, I decided to go pick up the kids. Since his parents were there, I didn't anticipate a problem. When we got ready to leave without Kevin he flew into a rage. He followed me to the door and started kicking and beating me in the foyer. It took his mother and his father to get him off of me. He constantly accused me of cheating and stated that he just couldn't take it anymore. After he finally calmed down, I talked to him for a while so that I could leave in peace.

Even though Kevin's behavior resembled a ticking time bomb, I still didn't turn him in to the police. I kept trying to convince myself that eventually he would get the picture and move on with his life. But in actuality, the more I rejected him, the more irate he became.

Chapter 6: "Trial and Errors"

I'm not exaggerating when I say that Kevin became a stalker in my life. Whether I saw him or not, he was always constantly watching me. He was following me— recording my every move. If he couldn't control my life when we were together, he was going to control it when we were apart.

My mother and I moved in together— ironically not far from the car dealership where Kevin used to and now returned to work. They gave him another company car and it wasn't long before Kevin showed up on the scene.

Sometimes he would be outside my job… watching me. Then he would call me at work—even though it was a violation of the court's protective order—and make threatening statements to me. He would tell me what I was wearing and what time I had arrived at work. I never saw him watching me. Not knowing where he was made me nervous. His moves got bolder and bolder each week. Then he became careless; one day he made a mistake that was almost fatal.

I was taking a nap before I went to work and was awakened by the telephone ringing. It was my next-door neighbor Sean. "Hey Whitney, what does your ex-husband look like?" I briefly described what Kevin looked like—and the kind of car he drove. The next thing I heard was the sounds of a fight. I ran to the window to see Kevin and Sean scuffling and rolling around on the sidewalk. Sean was an ex-convict who had served time for murder, so he was no stranger to conflict. Kevin tried to fight back, but he was no match for Sean.

In an instant, Sean had pulled out a gun and held it up to Kevin's temple. I heard him say with controlled rage, "Look man, she don't want you no more. Leave her alone! If you don't, I swear I will kill you. Do you understand me?" His words were slow and deliberate. He cocked the gun and spoke a little louder, "Don't ever let me catch you around here again. I just got out of prison for shooting a man, and I swear I'm not afraid to go back. Now get the hell out of here, and don't ever let me see you again."

For the first time since I had known Kevin, he was truly scared for his life. Now he knew how I felt every day. As he went back to his car, I saw that his pants were wet in the front and soiled in the back. Sean had literally 'scared the shit out of him.'

That run-in with Sean only affected him for a short period of time. Although he didn't come back to my house, he would still find other ways to harass me. In November of 1998, I was driving to work and saw Kevin following me in the rearview mirror. He pulled up beside me and motioned for me to roll down the window. I shook my head "no" and hoped he would go away. Although I couldn't hear him, I saw him mouth the words, "I'm gonna kill you." Then he hit the gas and swerved the car toward mine and tried to run me off the road. He followed me for miles, driving like a crazed maniac. I tried to get away by dodging between cars and eventually getting on the highway, but he stayed right on my tail trying to hit the rear bumper and make me pull off on the side of the road.

Other cars had to get out of the way just to keep from hitting—or getting hit—by us. I was driving recklessly, and so was he. In the mirror I watched as he continued to point and threaten me. I kept seeing him repeatedly say the words, "I'm gonna kill you." I was terrified.

I took an exit off the highway to head to the police station, but that put me right in the middle of a traffic jam. I had nowhere else to go. Fortunately, another motorist had witnessed what was happening and held up his cell phone to say he was calling the police. I nodded my head and then steered the car sharply up the curb and onto the front lawn of a business complex.

When my car stopped, Kevin pulled up beside me, jumped out and shouted. "I just want to talk to you,

Whitney. Get out of the car and let me talk to you!" I made sure I kept the car running and the doors locked. Then I hit the gas to get back into traffic, and he jumped onto the back of my car.

The traffic was moving ahead slowly, but I was going fast enough so that Kevin couldn't hold on. When I looked into the rearview mirror, I saw his body hit the pavement, roll for several feet, and then stop. I immediately thought, "Oh my God, I've killed him."

I slammed on the brakes and put the car in park. I sat for a moment looking in the side mirror to see if he was moving. I don't know which scared me more—the thought that I had killed him, or the thought that I hadn't. Slowly, I opened the car door and got out.

Several other motorists who had witnessed him jump onto the car and fall off had also pulled over and were walking toward him to see if he was OK. I called out to some of the bystanders as I slowly walked toward him, "Is he OK? Did I kill him? Did I hurt him?"

Kevin just lay there, but his eyes were watching me come closer. He was lying facedown and one arm was twisted underneath his body. One of his shoes had been knocked off from the fall. When I got within 25 feet of him, Kevin jumped up and ran towards me. I screamed and ran back to my car. I slammed and locked the car door and started the ignition—all in one motion. I threw the car into gear and hit the gas—barreling my way back into the rush-hour traffic.

Coming from the opposite direction a police officer was heading to the scene. I did a U-turn in the middle of the road and went back to the scene of the accident. I rolled down my window and frantically told the police officer, "That's my husband. He was trying to kill me. Please arrest him because he tried to kill me." I never did get out of the car. When the officer came toward me to find out what was going on, Kevin hopped back into his car to continue the chase. The police officer drew his weapon and chased him down on foot. I got away by running a couple of red lights and finally made it to the police station where I informed them about the incident. I also showed them copies of the protective order that had been filed against him.

When I got to the police station the officer already had Kevin in custody and was just about to release him.

Kevin had made up more lies, telling them it was a case of 'road rage' that had gotten out of hand, and that he had never seen me before. He made a convincing argument until they presented him with the protective order.

Once again, he was arrested for the weekend, and once again his parents came to bail him out. It was like a never-ending cycle that never worked in my favor.

Although I had left Kevin, he still found a way to ruin my life in a different way each and every day. There was something eerie about the way our relationship had deteriorated into the recent spate of madness. We were no longer a couple that was separated. We were enemies on opposing sides of the line. And in the game we were playing, it was kill or be killed. And the rules were always changing. Kevin bore no resemblance to the man I once loved.

December 4, 1998 will forever remain etched into my mind. Kevin continued his routine of calling and harassing me, but not as much that particular night. He had called me and stated he had gotten off work and was heading home. I was getting off shortly after that call.

My shift was almost over so I decided to take off my pantyhose because they had been itching and irritating me all night. It was late and cold outside. Kell and two other female co-workers walked out of the building with me. Because of the protective order, I was able to park right outside the building, so I offered to drive the three of them to their cars at the top of the hill.

We all got in and drove across the parking lot. When I went over the first speed bump, I noticed that my trunk light came on. That struck me as odd, because I hadn't been in my trunk all day. Kell said, "I hope that crazy ex-husband of yours hasn't tampered with your car and planted a bomb in it." We all laughed because they knew that lately Kevin had been acting crazier than usual.

When we went over the second speed bump, the light came on again, and we agreed to check it out once we got to their parked cars. One of the women with us got out along with Kell and tried to open the trunk. I pulled the trunk release lever, but nothing happened. When they pulled on the trunk again, Kevin jumped out and everybody started running and screaming. I jumped out of the car and started running to get away.

I kicked off my high-heeled shoes, but the pavement was cold and it cut into my bare feet. So, I just ran around the car trying to keep away from Kevin. One of the supervisors from work came running over because he saw Kevin jump out of the trunk. There was mass confusion. Kevin started pulling at his pants as if he had a gun, and I was afraid that he was going to hurt my co-workers, my friends and me. He demanded that I go with him, so I agreed.

"Whitney, don't go with him," they begged me. "You don't know what he's gonna do to you. Please don't go anywhere."

I was practically begging Kevin, "Please just leave my friends alone. They don't have anything to do with this. I'll go with you, but please don't hurt anyone else.

Just leave them out of this." He agreed, and I got in the car.

Kevin took off driving and was speeding out of the parking lot. My supervisor tried to jump in the car, and Kevin almost hit and killed him with his reckless driving. I screamed for him to slow down and tried to grab the steering wheel.

He just ignored my words and then dug his thumb into my eye to punish me. The car swerved across two lanes of traffic and I literally feared for my life. In the back of my mind I thought, "Tonight is the night that I'm going to die. One way or the other, my life is going to end."

By now, Kell had jumped into his car and had contacted the police on his cell phone. He followed us as Kevin sped down the highway. Kell tried to keep up and give the police our exact location. He caught up to us and flicked the lights as a warning. But that only enraged Kevin and he sped off even faster. As our speed approached 90 mph, Kevin's anger increased as well. He just screamed at me, "Look what you made me do. This is all your fault. I just wanted to talk to you. If you had just talked to me, we wouldn't have had to go through all this. Do you see what you've turned me into?" I yelled back at him, "Why don't you just stop the car? You're only making this situation worse, Kevin. Just stop now before you completely ruin both of our lives. Just stop the car. Do you hear me? Stop the damn car!"

He kept weaving down the road and eventually got off on a dark exit that wove through a residential neighborhood. He turned down a couple of side streets to evade Kell. Kevin made a quick, sharp turn into a neighborhood subdivision, and Kell's car kept speeding straight by. Now, the police wouldn't know where to find us. My only hope was to try and reason with Kevin and help him to calm down.

By now, Kevin had slowed down and was just driving aimlessly through the city. He saw a fast-food restaurant and pulled into the parking lot behind the building. He stopped the car and made me get out with him. All I could think about was the fact that nobody knew where I was, so this was the place where he was going to end it all. Out of desperation, I blurted out, "Are you going to kill me? Is that why you stopped? Are you going to kill me?" Tears streamed down my face, and my voice was quivering—as much from fear as from the frigid temperature. Frustration and anger were beginning to subside, and reality started to set in. I could tell by the look in his eyes that Kevin finally realized he had crossed the line, and that there was no turning back.

He had a blank look in his eyes, and he asked if I wanted him to carry me. That enraged me, "No, I don't want you to carry me. I don't want anything from you! What is wrong with you, Kevin? Are you crazy? Why are you doing this? Are you planning to kill me?" He didn't answer. He just made me keep walking further into the darkness.

Chill bumps covered my body, and I began to shiver. My feet were bruised from running in the parking lot earlier that night and walking barefoot in the cold. Kevin seemed to be retreating into his own little world, so I tried to reason with him and let him know the consequences of his actions if he didn't stop right then.

I told him that if he killed me, he would go to jail. I told him that our children—whom he loved so much— would be without a mother and a father. He loved those kids, so I tried to play on his sympathy using the kids. I tried everything I could think of to save my life. Kevin had stopped arguing and stopped talking to me at this point. I had no way of knowing what he was thinking. So, I just started to cry.

We walked down a narrow space with a long drop behind an abandoned warehouse and sat down near the edge of the woods. Kevin looked at me and said, "Take off your clothes." It was freezing outside. I thought to myself that he was going to rape me and then kill me;

and leave my body in the woods. The tone he used was not forceful or angry. As a matter of fact, he was gentler with me than he had ever been before. I said "no" and started to resist, but then I just lay very still and very quiet on the ground while he kissed me between my thighs, performed oral sex on me, and then had intercourse with me. As usual with him, "no" never meant "no."

When he finished, he realized what was happening and how out of control things had gotten, and he became angry all over again. Kevin began whispering and muttering to himself, "I should have taken the phone away from that guy. I really blew it this time. I'm going to be in so much trouble." I just sat quietly and listened to him while I put my clothes back on.

"Whitney, you should have just let me talk to you for a while. I wasn't going to hurt you—I just wanted to talk. Now look at what's happened. Why didn't I take the phone away from that guy at your job? Damn, I'm in a whole lot of trouble. I did all of this for you. I ruined my whole life because of you, Whitney. Damn."

Kevin went on to tell me that when he called me earlier and said he was going home, he honestly was. He said that he had gone to get some dinner and had a choice to make a right turn and go home or a left turn and come to my job—and try talking to me once more. He stated that when he got to my job, he started digging in the trunk of my car looking for evidence that I was sleeping with another man.

He decided that since I wouldn't talk to him on the phone, he would hide in the trunk. And when I got in the car, he planned to crawl through the back seat and talk to me face to face. Kevin's plan backfired when my co-workers got in the back seat and locked him in the trunk. He realized he should have made the right turn and gone home.

The charges just kept piling up. Kevin still hadn't faced the charges for jumping on the back of my car or violating his probation and the restraining order. Now, on top of everything else, he was facing kidnapping, rape and sexual assault charges. We sat out in the cold for three hours with Kevin—talking mostly to himself—trying to figure out how to make the best out of a very bad situation. He talked about stealing a car and leaving town to hide out. He was really grasping at straws. In the distance we heard a train whistle blowing, so then he decided that he should just end it all by jumping in front of the train. My mind was stuck on the fact that he was probably planning to kill me—and make good on the litany of threats he had been making over the years.

It's amazing how we all start out with these wonderful plans and aspirations for our lives. And it only takes one wrong decision to ruin it all. For Kevin, his mistakes were not taking "no" for an answer and refusing to get the help he clearly needed. For me, my mistake was expecting Kevin to change into someone he wasn't. I kept looking and waiting for my Prince Charming to show up again, but he never did.

While Kevin paced up and down near the edge of the woods, my mind drifted back to my childhood and teenage years. I thought about all the fun things I had missed out on. I remembered all the friends I didn't hang out with because I wanted to spend time with Kevin. I thought about all the things I didn't get to experience because I was in a relationship with him. I thought about all the things I would do differently if I had a chance to live my life over again. I figured these thoughts were the equivalent of "my life passing before my eyes." That night, I truly believed he was going to kill me.

I could hear my children's voices echoing in the back of my mind. I wasn't ready to leave them, and I definitely wasn't ready to die. They needed their mother, and I needed to be with them too. But Kevin had hurt me so badly in the past; killing me didn't seem to be out of the realm of possibility.

The Price of Love   by T.Bagley; Second Edition

It's interesting how we view situations when we think we may not get another chance to make things right. I just wanted to live. But the look in Kevin's eyes told me that he didn't care whether either one of us lived or died.

Kevin stopped pacing long enough to ask me a coherent question: "Will you help me?"

I hesitated. "Yes, I'll help you," I said. "I'll do everything I can to help you."

My survival instincts kicked in, and the balance of power began to shift.

I went behind that warehouse feeling frightened and afraid. But I emerged confident and secure in the fact that Kevin was no longer going to control my life. I knew he was scared, and I used that to my advantage. I played off of his vulnerabilities and regained his trust.

"Kevin, I'm here for you," I said. "Everything is going to be fine. I will help you however I can. Just trust me… everything is going to be OK." I gave Kevin a hug—not knowing it would be our last.

We walked back toward the car. Ever so slowly, the situation was beginning to lean toward my favor; the control had shifted onto my side. My main objective was to get away from that warehouse alive, and get back to the car and to a public place where somewhere else could see us. When we got back to the car, we noticed that the fuel level was on empty.

We stopped for gas at an all-night station, but it was closed for renovations. We kept driving until we got to another station, and we stopped to get gas. Kevin got out to pump the gas and I stayed in the car. My mind was going a mile a minute not knowing what to do next. As soon as Kevin got back in the car, a police cruiser drove up behind us; a wave of relief washed over me.

The officer didn't turn on his lights or the siren. He just followed us from a safe distance. Kevin kept driving and then started to speed up. He started going faster and faster saying he didn't want to go to jail over and over again. I said, "Kevin, you know he's calling for back-up. This is where it ends. Just put an end to this."

After he was convinced that I would keep him from going to jail, Kevin decided to pull over. With the car stopped and the engine still running, I put the car in park. Just as the officer was approaching the car, Kevin threw the car in gear, said he couldn't go to jail again, and sped off.

I yelled at him, "What are you doing? You've really made that officer mad!" When I turned around, I saw several police cars and they all had on blue lights and sirens. Kevin led chase for a few miles. At that point, I was more afraid of him having an accident and killing me than anything else. He took us down a two-lane highway with the officers following close behind.

Ahead of us was a roadblock with police officers from three different districts. I told Kevin to just stop the car and give up. I told him he wasn't getting through the blockade, so he needed to give up. Kevin had to reassure himself one final time that I would help get him out of this situation, and I told him I would. Finally, it was over. Once again Kevin stopped the car, and I put the car in park. The next thing we heard was a booming voice on a megaphone, "You in the car—get your hands up."

I had never seen so many guns drawn in my life. A police officer slowly opened my door, grabbed me and threw me on the ground out of the way. Emotion swept over me like a flood, and I just lay there on the ground crying. I was finally free.

When we got to the police station I was told that my mother had been contacted and was on her way. Shortly after my mother and Kell arrived, I went to give my statement to an officer. I described everything that had happened in full detail except the actual rape and sexual assault. I looked at my mother and said, "and of course he made me do it."

To this day, I will never forget that officer asking me whether or not I said "no." I did. I had said "no" many

times. The officer looked at me and said, "he raped you."
For the first time in my entire 10-year relationship with
Kevin I realized that he was raping me every time I said
"no"—and he forced me to have sex anyway. At that
very moment, I realized six out of my seven
pregnancies—including my three living children—were
conceived in rape, not love. That realization tore me
apart on the inside.

Once I was through at the police station I was taken to
the local hospital. I was treated for my eye, and my
swollen and cut feet; but mainly I was there to have a
rape kit prepared on me. The local battered women's
shelter sent an advocate to the hospital to support me
during that trying time. I can remember not saying too
much of anything because I was so exhausted. All I
wanted to do was go to bed.

Later that day Kevin was arrested and charged with
multiple charges. Since he had been arrested so many
other times prior to this one and gotten out, the judge
finally saw that he was clearly a danger to me. Kevin's
bail was set at $500,000.

Kevin's parents tried to put up their house up in Virginia
to get him out on bail, but luckily they couldn't put up
out-of-state property. A couple of months later, Kevin's
bail was lowered to $250,000. His parents couldn't come

up with the money, so Kevin remained in jail until we went to trial in August 2000.

After Kevin's indictment his parents realized that he was facing serious prison time and showed their true colors. They turned on me and made everything out to be my fault. Mrs. Little had now stopped talking to me altogether. On the other hand, if it wasn't Kevin calling me, it was his dad—begging me to get the charges dropped. But the state had so much evidence against Kevin that they didn't even need me to press charges. In fact, all of the charges against Kevin were listed as the State of North Carolina vs. Kevin Little—not Whitney Little vs. Kevin Little. I couldn't help Kevin if I wanted to. It was out of my hands and I no longer felt any of it was my fault.

I had given Kevin more chances than any one person deserved. I had held up my end of the bargain and stayed with him through thick and thin; richer or poorer, sickness and health, and I put up with things I wouldn't wish on my worst enemy. Even though I had gone through all of that, I still didn't want to see Kevin go to prison. I still wish things had turned out differently. I realized that Kevin made his own decisions, and now he had to deal with the consequences.

The night before we went to court, I had the same recurring nightmare, but this time the ending was different. In my dream, I saw a shadowy figure in the corner, and he started walking toward me with a knife.

I yelled out "NO" at the top of my lungs, and he ran away. I sat up gasping for air and clutching the side of my bed. Then I felt a calm all around me and knew that everything was going to be OK.

We spent two weeks in court testifying about the past 10 years of my life. It was the world and me against Kevin Little.

Judge: "Ladies and gentlemen, you've been sworn and impaneled to serve as a juror in this case. At this time, I'd like to explain to you the manner in which we will proceed as we seek together to find the truth.

First of all, the lawyers will have an opportunity to make opening statements to you. The purpose of an opening statement is narrow and limited. It is a mere forecast of what that attorney believes the admissible evidence will show during the course of the trial. An opening statement is not evidence. It must not be considered by you to be evidence.

The evidence will come in the form of the testimony of the witnesses, any admissions of the parties, stipulations of counsel, or any physical exhibits that may be offered by the parties.

Following the opening statement evidence will be offered and witnesses will be placed under oath and questioned by the attorneys.

When the evidence is complete, the lawyers will make their final argument to you. Again, the final arguments from the attorneys are not evidence, but are given to assist you in evaluating the evidence that you've heard during the course of the trial. Finally, just before you retire to consider your verdict, I will give you my instructions on the law that you are to apply to the facts in this case. At that time, I will declare and explain to you the law arising on the evidence. Then you will be taken to the jury room to deliberate upon your verdict."

The first few days were a reiteration of all the abuse that had taken place over the years. This gave the jury background information to see and understand the pattern of abuse that had developed. I guess my testimony was so powerful that Kevin's attorney had convinced him to accept a plea three different times during the trial—but he backed out every time. He had a chance to get less jail time if he had just pleaded guilty, but he was confident that he would be acquitted of all charges.

Kevin's parents were in court everyday supporting their son. They never spoke to me. In fact, when I was giving my testimony Mrs. Little ignored me and flipped through a magazine. And when I started giving damaging testimony, they both sat in the courtroom taunting me. They were so distracting that the judge ordered them to stop or he would hold them in contempt of court.

The next couple of days featured various witnesses who testified about random attacks and Kevin's erratic behavior right before his arrest. Psychologists and forensic psychiatrists who provided information about Kevin's mental state dominated the second week of testimony.

Kevin had been diagnosed with bipolar disorder, and his attorneys were hoping to use that diagnosis to their advantage to keep him out of jail. The first physician testified: "Bipolar illness is really manifested on a spectrum. One end of the spectrum is severe major depression during which a person can be suicidal.

They're not eating, not sleeping, crying constantly, and show no energy. The other end of the spectrum is kind of the opposite of that—where they may have excessive energy, not require any sleep, sometimes going on spending sprees or demonstrating bad periods of judgment. Often substance abuse is part of this. When I first met Kevin, I think he'd been tried on a couple of antidepressants. The standard treatment for bipolar illness is basically a mood stabilizer. Lithium was the first mood stabilizer. Since that time, we have several others. We also commonly use anti-psychotic medications, and these are usually to treat delusions or hallucinations, which are also very common in the manic state of this illness.

The nature of bipolar illness is quite variable. There are forms known as rapid recycling where a person's mood can change over the course of an hour or two, and that's just the run of the mill bipolar disorder where recycling is usually every three to four months. The longer it goes untreated, usually the harder it is to treat and the more frequent the relapses are.

In dealing with Kevin Little, we observed and treated him in a mixed state. That means the person has manifestations of both depression and mania at the same time."

Throughout the trial, it was evident that Kevin still didn't believe he had done anything wrong. His whole defense was "how can a husband rape his own wife?" He still was unwilling to accept responsibility for his actions, and it showed. As his fate was drawing nearer, he motioned cutting my throat from ear to ear. He didn't have a lot of sympathizers during the trial. As a matter of fact, his arrogance and nonchalance toward the proceedings irritated the judge and his own attorney. He just didn't get it.

Before it was all over, Kevin had angered his now second defense attorney. Kevin's first set of attorneys quit right before the trial started because they couldn't deal with his tactics, and his current attorney couldn't seem to get the trial over quickly enough.

Judge: "Members of the jury, you've heard the evidence and the argument of counsel for the State and the defendant. It is your duty not only to consider all the evidence, but to consider all the arguments and the contentions and positions urged by the State's attorneys and the defense attorney, and any other contention arising from the evidence; and to weigh them in light of your common sense and as best as you can, determine the truth in this matter.

I instruct you that a verdict is not a verdict until all 12 jurors agree unanimously as to what your decision shall be. You all have a duty to consult with one another and to deliberate with a view to reaching an agreement, if it can be done without violence to your individual judgment. Each of you must decide the case for yourself, but only after an impartial consideration of the evidence with your fellow jurors."

The time had come for Kevin to face both judge and jury: Judge: "Ladies and gentleman of the jury, I'm told you have a verdict. Is that correct?"

Jury: "Yes."

Judge: "In file number 107818, you find the defendant Kevin Little guilty of felonious restraint. Is this your verdict, so say you all?"

Jury: "Yes."

Judge: "As to count two, your foreman has returned your verdict and you find the defendant guilty of assault on Whitney Jordan Little. Was this your verdict, so say you all?"

Jury: "Yes."

Judge: "As to count three, you find the defendant guilty of assault on Whitney Little. Is this your verdict, so say you all?"

Jury: "Yes."

Judge: "In file number 102414, your foreman has returned your verdict and you find the defendant guilty of careless and reckless driving. Was this your verdict, so say you all?"

Jury: "Yes."

Judge: "In file number 102406, your foreman has returned your verdict, and you find the defendant guilty of violating a domestic violence order. Is this your verdict, so say you all?"

Jury: "Yes."

Judge: "In file number 64575, as to one count, your foreman has returned your verdict and you find the defendant guilty of second-degree rape. Was this your verdict, so say you all?"

Jury: "Yes."

Judge: "As to count two, your foreman has returned your verdict, and you find the defendant guilty of second-degree sexual offense. Was this your verdict, so say you all?"

Jury: "Yes."

Out of all of the charges that Kevin was found guilty of, he wanted to know which jurors convicted him on the rape and sexual assault charges. So the jury was polled— and to Kevin's surprise—it was all of them. It was finally proven to him that a husband could rape his wife and go to jail for it also.

The jury was dismissed. The case had been made, and Kevin was found guilty. After two weeks of testimony, the 12-year ordeal was finally coming to an end. The

State prosecutor in her remarks during pre-sentencing, summed up the total of my experiences with Kevin:

"Your Honor, I don't want to be overly dramatic about this case, but this is a case where I think you as the sentencing judge literally hold this woman's life in your hands. Kevin Little wouldn't listen to anybody when they told him to leave Whitney Jordan Little alone. Judges tried to tell him with protective orders, but he wouldn't listen. They tried to get through to him with release orders from the jail. He still didn't listen.

A next-door neighbor held a gun to his head and said, "Leave her alone." He didn't do it. He wouldn't listen to anybody. He's not going to be deterred if he's out of prison. That's a fact.

Your Honor, you've had an opportunity to observe his behavior in this courtroom. He doesn't accept responsibility for anything that he did. He will never get it. I know this sounds dramatic, but if he's out of prison, then she's in danger. And for that reason Your Honor, I would request that he be sentenced consecutively for each of the felony charges and that he be sentenced in the aggravated range. That's the only way that the State can say in good faith that we've done our job and that we've asked you to do what we think will protect her."

The judge gave Kevin a chance to speak before he received his sentence: He said, "I just wish things could

have worked out differently. We could have perhaps
settled things between us in a marriage counselor's
office instead of a court of law. Now I just want to go
home and be with my children. That's all. That's my
whole intent. I don't want to get out and cause my ex-
wife any undue harm, any undue stress, or anything of
that nature. I want to get out and be with my kids.

This has been a difficult adjusting period for me, and I'm
not looking forward to spending time in prison. I just
want to reiterate that I don't wish her any harm. I wish
her no harm at all, and I'm glad to know that she's doing
well. I don't want to get out and hurt her again, or
anything to that effect. As I stated earlier, I just want to
get out and be a father to my kids.

They need a father in their lives. If I were released today,
all I would do is run and get my children and try to make
up for all the lost time. I wouldn't go out and commit
some foolish act that would land me back in jail. I don't
wish her any harm at all. I'm just concerned about my
kids. I love my children more than anything in this
world."

The judge responded before he announced the sentence:

"Well Mr. Little, this is a sad situation. Of course, you're
the master of your fate. You're here because of your
actions. You've had decisions to make during this

proceeding. You've had decisions to make in life, and because of those decisions, you stand here in front of me today. As I have said, my primary concern is for your ex-wife, and I don't want anything to happen to her. I'm not totally convinced that you see the occurrences about which you stand in here facing me today as being your fault. It seems you're not accepting the responsibility that I'd like to see you accept for your actions. And I feel that your ex-wife is just not safe from you at this point. The only thing I can do is follow my instincts and render your judgment accordingly.

Before rendering Kevin's sentence the courtroom filled with sheriff deputies for everyone's protection.

Kevin was sentenced to a minimum of 73 months and a maximum of 97 months in a federal prison. He was due for release in December 2004.

The judge asked me if I had anything to say:

Whitney's Statement:

"All I can say is that I'm sorry; I'm sorry that it had to come to this. I hate it for my kids mainly, because of their relationship with their father—Kevin. And like I said in my testimony, my kids were the main reason I stayed with him. It's tough to raise three children alone, but I'm doing it. I've been doing it alone, and I'll continue to do it alone. This may sound harsh, but as far as I'm concerned, he's the one who made the decision to not be a part of his kids' lives when he did what he did to me. I've done everything I can do for this man. I have been with him for so long, and I've put up with so much stuff that nobody knows about. I used to feel really guilty and like somehow things were my fault. And even though he did horrible, horrible things to me, I forgave him anyway because I loved him. But I think I'm finally coming to the point that I realize he has to take responsibility for his own actions. I'm just sorry that it came to this, and I'm really sorry that Kevin didn't try to get the help he needed. I just wish he would have listened—if not to me—to somebody.

I want to apologize to my children, because I know how much we hurt them. I wish that things could have been different. I'm sorry they had to witness the violence and abuse in our home, and I'm sorry they had to grow up so fast and deal with adult issues—even though they're still so young. I love my children more than anything in this world, and I would do anything to protect them. I'm just glad that this nightmare has finally come to an end.

To the reporters covering this trial, I'd like them to let the world know that domestic violence is real, and it's a serious issue facing this nation. Women all over this country are prisoners in their own homes. It's up to you

The Price of Love   by T.Bagley; Second Edition

to educate your readers and listeners about domestic violence.

I want to thank everyone who testified in this trial on my behalf and tell everyone who stood by my side how much I appreciate them. There were days when I thought I wasn't going to make it. There were days when I didn't want to wake up and face another day. I didn't want to become a statistic. I didn't want to be divorced. I didn't want my children to grow up without their father. I didn't want to become a single mother raising three children by herself. And I definitely didn't want to send another young man to prison. But this is the hand that has been dealt to me, and I'm playing it everyday.

I'm a fighter. And today, I'm a winner. That's all I have to say."

Works Cited

D. Ashley Hill, M.D. "Issues and Procedures in Women's Health" (online article)

http://www.OBGYN.net. Department of Obstetrics and Gynecology: Florida Hospital Family Practice Residency; Orlando, Florida

Interact of Wake County

www.interactofwake.org

PRINTHOUSE BOOKS

Read it, Enjoy it, Tell A Friend!

PrintHousebooks.com

The Price of Love   *by T.Bagley; Second Edition*

CPSIA information can be obtained
at www.ICGtesting.com
Printed in the USA
FSHW02n2314011018
52528FS

9 780988 642867